SWANAGE ENCYCLOPAEDIC G·U·I·D·E

with the author's best wishes

Rodney Legg

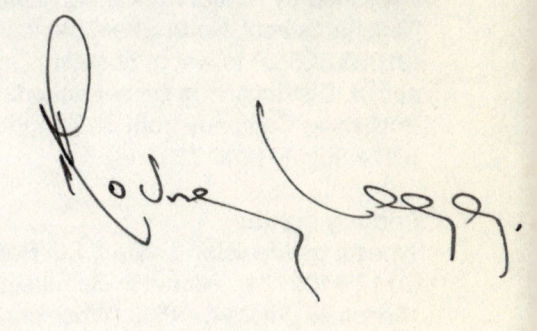

Rodney Legg [signature]

dpc
Dorset Publishing Company
WINCANTON PRESS, NATIONAL SCHOOL, NORTH STREET
WINCANTON, SOMERSET BA9 9AT

For **Richard Duke**
who found his "Burmah"
roots on the Great Globe

Publishing details
First published 1995. Copyright Rodney Legg © 1995
Published by Dorset Publishing Company at the Wincanton Press, National School, North Street, Wincanton, Somerset BA9 9AT (01963 32583) to whom updatings may be sent, addressed to the author. Distribution in Dorset undertaken by Maurice Hann of the Dorset Publishing Company from 36 Langdon Road, Parkstone, Poole, Dorset BH14 9EH (01202 738248).

Printing credits
Typeset by Mediatec Limited, PO Box 738, London SW19 1TY (0117 9409134). Printed in Somerset by Bookcraft at Units 5-12, Midsomer Enterprise Park, Wheelers Hill, Midsomer Norton, Bath BA3 2BX (01761 419167).

Restrictions upon copying
All rights reserved. No part of this publication may be reproduced, stored in a retrieval system, or transmitted in any form or by any means, electronic, computerised, mechanical, photocopying, recording or otherwise, without prior permission in writing from the copyright owner.

International standard book number
ISBN 0 948699 45 0

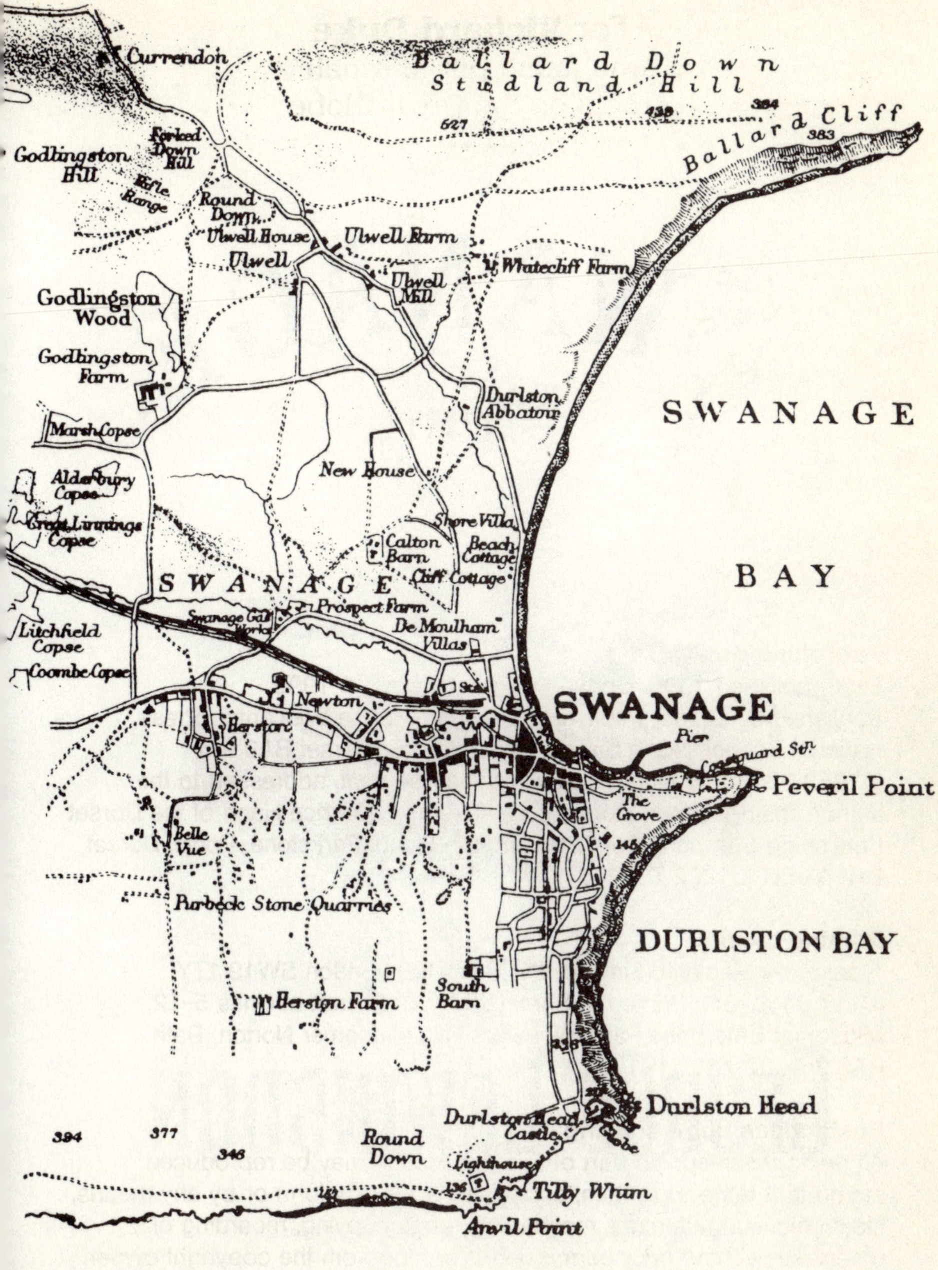

Currendon
Ballard Down
Studland Hill
627
439
384
383
Ballard Cliff
Forked Down Hill
Godlingston Hill
Rifle Range
Round Down
Ulwell House
Ulwell Farm
Ulwell
Whitecliff Farm
Ulwell Mill
Godlingston Wood
Godlingston Farm
Durlston Abbatoir
Marsh Copse
SWANAGE
New House
Alderbury Copse
Shore Villa
Calton Barn
Beach Cottage
Cliff Cottage
BAY
SWANAGE
Prospect Farm
Swanage Gas Works
De Moulham Villas
Litchfield Copse
Coombe Copse
Newton
SWANAGE
Herston
Pier
Coastguard Stn
Peveril Point
The Grove
146
Belle Vue
Purbeck Stone Quarries
DURLSTON BAY
South Barn
Herston Farm
Durlston Head
Durlston Head Castle
394
377
346
Round Down
Lighthouse
136
Tilly Whim
Anvil Point

DEDICATED BY PERMISSION TO
GEORGE BURT ESQ[RE].
SHERIFF OF LONDON AND MIDDLESEX.

SWANAGE,
Song.

Written and Composed

BY

GEORGE LEWINGDON.

Author of
LIFT UP THE ROYAL STANDARD & *SONG* BOURNEMOUTH.

Price 3s/-

PUBLISHED BY
GEORGE LEWINGDON.
SWANAGE.

1. Sa_lu_brious air of Swanage, How glad it makes one feel Fresh fields and pas_tures deck'd with green, The weak it soon will heal The charm_ing beach of Swan_age bay From

2. The chalk_y cliffs at Bollard head The Gull and Corm_'rants home Where Har_ry and his wife both stand With gran_deur in the foam The dark blue wa_ter rush_ing by With

stone and shingle free With lofty
ebb and flowing tide Where vessels

hills of Colour'd sand And a deep refreshing
lay in western gales And all in safety

sea.
ride.

3. At Pev-'ril point a dou-ble reef Of jag-ged rocks are seen And there you find the u-nio beds with spar both red and green 'Twas here the Dan-ish ships were sunk For

4. Near to this is Durl-stone head A splen-did fore-land there Where rug-ged rocks in bold re-lief Stand tow-'ring in the air There's Til-ly whim and An-vil cove What

his-t'ry tells us so A glo-rious
charm-ing spots to see Where smug-glers

vic-t'ry Eng-land won A thou-sand years a-
hid their bran-dy kegs From off the deep blue

go.
sea.

HMS *Abel Tasman* - manned by eleven members of the Royal Navy Volunteer Reserve and returning empty from St Valery, where she had been helping the evacuation of remnants of the British and French armies, this vessel hit a mine in the Swash Channel at the entrance to Poole Harbour [13 June 1940].

She was blown to pieces and all aboard were killed. One crewman, Ordinary Seaman E.J.H. Gosling, aged 20, is buried in Swanage Cemetery, Washpond Lane, Godlingston.

Adams - de facto ruler of Penang **Lieutenant-Colonel Sir Arthur (Robert) Adams** [1861-1937] retired from Malaya to Rockleigh on Peveril Point. He only had short-term direct rule over the colony's Eastern Archipelago [1910-11] but frequently exercised longer and wider power as Solicitor-General of Penang and Commandant of the Penang Volunteers [1899-1919].

Air-raids - German bombs fell on Swanage in the Second World War, with 1942 being the year that saw most hit-and-run raids by the Luftwaffe. Historian and author Merle Chacksfield of Rabling Road has provided the following list of the major incidents in 1942.

20 April: Houses damaged in Cornwall Road and commercial buildings in Station Road.

13 July: Three people injured and houses damaged, mostly in Park Road.

14 May: Bomb damage to historic Wesley's Cottage [*see its entry*]. This was later demolished and its commemorative stone found its way to Fontmell Magna, though its return to Swanage was being arranged in 1993.

17 August: Eight people killed and thirty-nine wounded. The Westminster Bank at 1 Institute Road suffered a direct hit and was destroyed. Miss Helen Muspratt's photographlc studio at 10 Institute Road was badly damaged, as was Hayman's Cafe. Bombs also fell in The Narrows, the constricted terraces of old cottages in the middle of the High Street, and in Chapel Lane and Church Hill. Cottages opposite the old parish churchyard were ruined and part of the tile roof taken off St Mary's Church. There was also damage to the nearby Tithe Barn.

23 August: Five people killed and nine wounded. Extensive damage caused to the commercial buildings around The Square. The most dramatic casualty was the monumental terracotta cow that was the centrepiece of the facade to Swanage Dairies, lying in pieces amid the rubble of the collapsed building. The adjoining Ship Inn also suffered considerable damage.

Albert the Good - monument erected by John Mowlem [1862] in the High Street above Court Hill, in memory of Prince Albert, Queen Victoria's consort [1819-61], who had visited Swanage [1849].

The obelisk part of the structure was taken down in the 1930s and the base, with its inscription to "ALBERT THE GOOD" and his dates, was demolished after a dispute with developers in 1971. I rediscovered it, stacked in sections, in St Aldhelm's Quarry near St Alban's Head [1992].

J.G. Harrod's *Directory of Dorsetshire* for 1865 has fulsome praise for "The Albert Memorial":

"Small as Swanage is at present, it has displayed, in proportion to its limits, a highly loyal patriotic feeling. In doing justice to the memory of Albert the Good, the inhabitants were amongst the foremost. A very chaste and well-proportioned obelisk, with an appropriate inscription, was erected by the north side of the road above the Cemetery, at a point where it is seen for a considerable distance in either direction of the highway, and at once forms a beautiful foreground object to the view of the valley, and a very interesting one in all the views from it."

Alexandrovna - 1,250-ton Liverpool sailing ship disabled by a hurricane in the English Channel in the early hours of Saturday 29 April 1882. As the winds lessened the vessel was reported missing. That afternoon, however, she drifted in towards the newly operational lighthouse south of Swanage, with her topsails in ribbons and only a staysail set.

No crew were seen and in minutes "the fated ship was among the broken billows which covered the sea with foam for hundreds of yards from the rocks". She struck the perpendicular cliff half a mile west of Anvil Point, on the Ragged Rocks to the west of Round Down. In ten minutes, when the rescuers had run along the clifftop to the spot, she was in pieces and nothing was seen of the crew of seventy-seven. All were lost and many bodies were later found "jammed in among the rocks, or floating in the waters of the Channel, most of them bearing marks of frightful injuries - inflicted, it is to be hoped, after death".

The following Thursday evening the steamer *Empress* brought a large party from Bournemouth and Swanage round Durlston Head "to see the remnants of the sad wreck of the unfortunate vessel". They saw "immense quantities of wreck" including two large sections of the ship. One body was found naked with a lifebuoy in its arms and others were picked up "much bruised and disfigured".

Describing the hurricane, C.E. Robinson wrote that year: "The phenomenal violence of the gale may be judged from the fact that sea-salt is recorded to have been blown by it more than a hundred miles inland; and that it completely stripped all the trees in exposed situations on the coast of their young green leaves, which the spring had just brought out. The elms at Swanage were not covered with leaf again until past midsummer."

All Saints Church - in Ulwell Road, on the corner with Redcliffe Road, this suburban building of stone and pantiles is of simple design with only a cross for embellishment. Built by George Parsons of Swanage, in 1956-57, it cost £19,000.

Its treasure, a gift from parishioners at Bingham's Melcombe on the Dorset Downs, is an elegant classical font dated 1751, which has a circular bowl with bay-leaf ornamentation and a wooden pineapple finial.

Anchor Inn - eighteenth century bow-windowed hostelry with a long frontage on the north side of the High Street towards its seaward end, which was a place of style and pretentions long before the town became a popular resort.

Its gig-and-fly was the only public transport in early nineteenth century Swanage, though hardly a mass-transit vehicle given that the hire of it and the two horses, plus driver in leather and a red coat, would be at the then colossal price of 30 shillings for a ride to Wareham.

SWANAGE ENCYCLOPAEDIC GUIDE 4

The Anchor also provided the town's first bathing machine, though this again was restricted by price to the right class. One horse and a male attendant were necessary for its passage to the beach, and then a nurse to supervise its use and to ensure that everything was proper and decent. Watering in Swanage in the early nineteenth century cost the equivalent of a world cruise today.

Annie Margretta - 500-ton Norwegian timber schooner lost beneath Ballard Point, or Ballard Head as it was known, in the early hours of 24 January 1879. She was en route from France to the United States, as had been the much luckier *Constitution* which grounded only a few hundred yards away just a week before.

By afternoon, *Annie Margretta* was a total wreck. Assistance was late in coming from the Swanage lifeboat which itself encountered difficulty in launching down the Peveril slipway against the force of a heavy sea driven directly inshore by a strong easterly wind.

The Life-boat Institution decided as a result to build a groyne to hold back the waves. As for the wreck beneath Ballard Head, that was auctioned for £45.

Backwater to Herston - the fishing hamlet of Swanage used to cluster along the south side of an inlet and backwater that stretched inland, westwards for a mile. This was along the Brook, extending north into the area that would be transformed by the building of the railway line in 1884.

Houses on the north side of the High Street had gateways at the bottom of their gardens, on to the fishermen's moorings. These were worked with the tide and iron eye-rings have been discovered set in walls that are now considerable distances from the nearest water.

Some were at the Barley Mow and next to the Town Hall where the Drong was a narrow alley to the backwater. On the tide, stone barges were hauled upstream, to a loading point between central Herston and what is now King George's Field, in the region of Prospect Farm. Reputedly, at one time, there was a shipping wharf much further upstream, between Quince Hill Wood and the buildings at New Barn. This is two miles west of the town, on the 40 feet contour and well above help from the tides.

The seaward end of the Backwater is not that much easier to trace. Its mouth extended across the site of what is now the Mowlem and had a quay on the south side, where the Parade now stands. Here stood a pair of stone-roofed cottages that were partially washed away by the sea at 02.00 hours on 29 December 1848.

John Mowlem records in his diary that a fierce sea held back the tidal water in this backwater until "after three hours ebb-tide, such was the rush of water by the Brook that it undermined the foundation of a house in the occupation of Mr John Soper, master of the cutter *Gertrude*, that the front fell into the Brook and Mrs Soper fell with it. She was found [drowned] on the shore nearly opposite our house." Her two daughters and two female lodgers were "with great difficulty ... rescued by James Pushman and others".

The surge scoured the bed of the Brook which once more became a Backwater, expanding "from about 6 feet wide to 30 feet and upwards".

Ballard Down Obelisk - on the Swanage side of the hilltop parish boundary with Studland (Ordnance Survey map reference SZ 022 813), this has had an up and down history, being demolished in London, re-erected above the Ulwell Gap [1892], toppled over and was put up again [1893], and then deliberately dismantled because of its potential use as a navigation aid for German bombers [1940].

The white Devonshire granite obelisk was rebuilt in 1973. Its shaft had been scattered in five sections across the mound of a prehistoric round barrow, on which it had stood. The re-erection, at just below the 500-feet contour, was carried out in a few hours by a company of Royal Engineers from a summer camp at Weymouth. The idea had come from Bishop George Snow of Corfe Castle. When I told him a few weeks before that his request to Dorset's south-east planning sub-committee had been approved "subject to no adverse comment from the Department of the Environment" as a "minor departure from the coastal belt policy" he was delighted: "It is entirely a whim on my part but I have been trying for a long time to get this obelisk put up again. It was pulled down during the war because it was a landmark. As a child I came to Swanage year after year and I came to associate a whole landscape with it. Then one day we returned after the war was over and found it on the ground."

Brigadier John Snow, who died suddenly in February 1973, suggested to the bishop that the army could be persuaded to put it back on the skyline. "It will be done by sheer manpower and block and tackle alone," Bishop Snow explained to planning officials. "They will carry out a reconnaissance one day and do it the next."

The obelisk was erected on Ballard Down in 1892 by George Burt, the baron of Swanage's Victorian speculators, to mark the opening at the bottom of the hill of Ulwell reservoir which successfully extracted water from the chalk and was to have a profound effect on the town's land values and development potential. Pure water was first tapped from below these chalk hills in 1884.

The plinth is Purbeck stone, and the obelisk itself is in five sections of white marble. It had originally been a lamp standard, outside the church of St Mary Woolnoth on the corner of King William Street and Lombard Street in the City of London. When it was removed as an obstruction by the Swanage-owned firm of road-makers, John Mowlem and Company, it came with tons of other streetside junk to embellish Purbeck. In two of the sections of the obelisk, when they were strewn across the ground, you could see the iron pipe - going up the centre - which carried the gas to the lamp. One of these failed to be reset in the 1973 lifting operation and is still propped beside the plinth.

Beneath the obelisk, the eight feet high burial mound is itself a prominent bump on the skyline, and shows that Bronze Age man could also appreciate a landmark. A trussed-up skeleton was dug from the barrow by J.H. Austen in the mid-1800s and this disturbance probably accounts for the reputed instability of Burt's pillar.

Ballard Down Round Barrows - marked as tumuli on the map (Ordnance Survey references SZ 022 813, SZ 027 812 and SZ 040 813), these prehistoric burial mounds date from the Bronze Age. There are eight but only the western specimen, into which the Victorian Obelisk has been set, remains substantially intact as a prominent feature on the skyline.

This, the six feet high Ulwell Barrow, was opened by Victorian antiquary John Austen in 1857. He found a trussed-up skeleton in a chalk-cut grave, with a fine red-ware handled cup which would have held the drink for that journey to the after-world. An antler in the filling showed how the grave had been dug. There was another, later, skeleton inserted further up in the mound as well as urn fragments and a cremation beneath a stone. The mound is dated to between 2,100 and 1,500 BC.

To the east, also on National Trust land, the barrows have fared less well. They would also have covered aristocratic burials of the rich Wessex culture and had their visits from John Austen and his barrow diggers in 1851-57. The mounds were then quite sizeable but the eastern cluster were damaged in the Second World War, apparently for the construction of a coastal radar station, and all were denuded by subsequent ploughing for cereals, which was stopped when Whitecliff Farm was bought by the National Trust.

There was a primary burial of a single crouched skeleton beneath each mound, and as with Ulwell Barrow Austen found pieces of antler-pick which had been used to quarry the chalk. The mounds had then been re-used in the latter part of the Bronze Age for the insertion of cremation burials. The urns containing these had largely disintegrated. There was also the burial of a child in a pit that had been cut into the chalk.

Bartlett - rector **Rev Thomas Oldfeld Bartlett** [1786-1841] acquired the parish's first detached cemetery, as his stone there recorded: "21 YEARS THE BELOVED RECTOR OF THIS PARISH AND WORTH MATRAVERS HE DEPARTED THIS LIFE FEBRUARY 27, 1841, AGED 55 YEARS, AND WAS BY HIS OWN DESIRE INTERRED WITHIN THIS BURIAL GROUND, OBTAINED THROUGH HIS EXERTIONS AND CONSECRATED OCTOBER 12, 1826."

His new cemetery is on the slope opposite the south-east corner of the parish church. Not that his stone is there any longer; it has been moved to the north-east corner of the actual church, making a nonsense of the wording.

Bats - these mammals have a nationally-important stronghold in the Isle of Purbeck because of the extensive hiding and hibernation places offered by the quarry shafts and coastal workings. Purbeck has the widest range of species of bats in southern England and some of the densest populations. Care has to be taken in writing of these localities as most of the abandoned shafts have been at least partially blocked by dumped rubbish and the hibernating bats are especially vulnerable to vandalism. One malicious person can kill an entire population of hundreds of sleeping bats in less than an hour.

As an example of the other hazard, a colony of the Mouse-eared bat was discovered in a Purbeck quarry in 1956 but the entrance was then bulldozed and the bats disappeared. It was only the second record for the whole country though the bat has been seen in Dorset since.

No less than seventeen species of bat have been found in the cliff quarries at Winspit and these groups are being protected by naturalists. In the Swanage quarries in the 1940s, Bernard Gooch explored many underground lanes that have since been filled. He found that badgers, foxes and rabbits also used the deep shafts and measured a constant underground temperature of 50 degrees Fahrenheit, only lessened where air could circulate from one shaft to another, and the bats preferred the lower temperatures for hibernation. Gooch was told that bats spent the winter underground even when quarrymen were cutting stone in neighbouring galleries.

The rare Bechstein's bat was first discovered in Purbeck in 1947 and during the cold winter of that year, five hibernating Serotine bats were also found, the first time this common bat had been recorded from caves or mines in the British Isles. Gooch found the Greater Horseshoe to be the commonest bat underground.

In some quarry lanes he was surprised to find no bats on any visit, and noted that "these neglected or deserted lanes had one feature in common - rough, untidy quarry walls. The latter are generally neatly made of relatively large blocks of stone, or they may consist of solid rock, both of which the bats use, as well as the ceiling, when looking for somewhere to hang. Has this avoidance of lanes of rough, or rubbly, walls anything to do perhaps with the bats' echo-location requirements? Emitting a series of ultra-sonic squeaks as they fly along these pitch-dark lanes, they receive perhaps confusing or disconcerting echoes ... then naturally they might prefer to hang up in lanes where echo-location proves easiest. These rough lanes afford ample footholds and bats evidently fly along them."

Purbeck naturalist Leonard Tatchell was driven into a cave at Winspit, on the coast at Worth Matravers, by heavy rain. He found himself in a quarry that had not been worked for many years: "After getting accustomed to the semi-darkness I began to explore and, looking up I saw about a score of the Common Horseshoe bat, and going further in I found that the roof of this working was teeming with hundreds of the creatures, and the odour was not pleasant. I amused myself by throwing up small stones and got many of them flying."

The last sentence is no longer acceptable behaviour!

Baynes - aircraft designer and inventor **L.E. Jeffery ('Baron') Baynes** [1902-89] is buried in Swanage Cemetery, Washpond Lane, Godlingston. He built novel little flying machines such as an auxiliary sailplane with a Carden engine which, together with its propeller, could be retracted into the fuselage; as was displayed to the Royal Aeronautical Society meeting at Fairey's Heathrow aerodrome [5 May 1935].

He was pioneering ultra-lights, such as the two-seater, twin-engined Bee which was only 29 feet 10 inches in length and put into construction by Carden-Baynes Aircraft Ltd at Heston. The twin 40hp Carden-engined Baynes Bee was taken up by Hubert Broad on its maiden flight [April 1937]. It and similar frivolities would be squeezed from the sky by the gathering clouds of war.

The Baynes Bee, plus a finely sculpted head, are carved on his Purbeck marble gravestone at Godlingston.

Bell - short-tempered **Dr Andrew Bell** [1753-1832] was Swanage's eccentric and often absentee rector from 1801 to 1809. He had worked for the East India Company but ill-health forced his return to England, with a £25,000 fortune and a substantial pension. The Swanage living was little more than a formal position though Bell did introduce the women of Swanage to the trade of spinning flax and making straw-plaited bonnets. Bell's time at Swanage was generally marred by his unfortunate marriage, in 1800, to Agnes Barclay, which was depicted as persecution by De Quincey in his *Essay on Coleridge*.

The Dictionary of National Biography records: "Perhaps the most marked feature in Bell's character was his love of money."

His other interest was education and he was a strident self-publicist. In India in 1789 he had pioneered the teaching method of mutual instruction using the brighter eight-year-olds to teach the infants. It became known as "the Madras System".

His writings on his chosen subject began with *An Experiment in Education* [1797] and included *A Sermon on the Education of the Poor* [1807] and *A Sketch of a National Institution for Training up the Children of the Poor in the Principles of our Holy Religion and in Habits of Useful Industry* [1808].

Bell Street - road south off the High Street at Herston Cross, named for Dr Andrew Bell, the rector from 1801. St Mark's Church is at the north end, on the east side.

Belle Vue Cliffs - three orchid-rich clifftop fields, covering 51 acres, bought by the National Trust in 1976. They lie towards the south-west corner of the parish (Ordnance Survey map reference SZ 017 769), immediately west of Durlston Country Park, and are crossed by the coastal public footpath.

[See also the entries for the Alexandrovna, Half Moon and Ragged Rocks].

Belvedere - see entry for **Seymer Road**

Bicycle - the first recorded arrival in Swanage "of this new fashioned 'horse'," the machine now known as a Penny-farthing, took place in 1869. The rider was William Trask, whose father was a Yeovil blacksmith, who accomplished the distance of 48 miles from the south Somerset town in nine hours.

His bicycle was newly-made and the sight of this innovative form of transport caused considerable excitement to spectators of all ages: "Inhabitants have had few opportunities of studying the breed before and are greatly puzzled how the queer-looking apparatus is kept upright."

Biggs - escaped train robber **Ronnie Biggs** [born 1929] lived at Swanage [1960] three years before a Royal Mail train, the Glasgow to London express, was stopped at Sears Crossing, Linslade, Buckinghamshire [3am on 6 August 1963] and robbed of £2,631,684. Sixteen other villains were also involved in the heist.

Biggs served his criminal apprenticeship in Dorset: "I did a lot of burglaries and thefts and appeared at Dorchester Quarter Sessions, where I got eighteen months."

He would flee to Rio de Janiero, Brazil, after breaking out of Wandsworth prison [1965].

Bliss - composer **Sir Arthur Bliss** [1891-1975], Master of the Queen's Musick [from 1953] was patron of the Purbeck Festival of Music and attended concerts at St Mary's Church, Swanage, and Lady St Mary's Church, Wareham. His widow, Lady Bliss, continued to attend these events.

Blyton - children's author **Enid Blyton** [1897-1968] "always spent her holidays at Swanage". She spotted ex-guardsman Christopher Rone [1915-90], an archetypal village bobby, who did a spell on his bicycle in the lanes around Studland.

Rone was immortalised as PC Plod in the *Noddy* stories. He retired to 1 Carey Close, Wareham, and died in the town.

Enid Blyton and her husband, Harley Street surgeon Kenneth Darrell-Waters, bought the Isle of Purbeck Golf Club [1951-65]. This lies on former Bankes estate land, now National Trust owned, on the Studland side of the Ulwell Gap.

Miss Blyton occasionally worked on her books on a table outside the clubhouse, which was then affectionately known as the "little tin hut", K. Merle Chacksfield records in its centenary publication *100 Years of Golf on the Isle of Purbeck* [1992]. This clubhouse stood on the left side of the Swanage to Studland road at Dean Hill, a short distance past the fork leading uphill towards Corfe Castle.

She took an active part in the life of Swanage and was for many years president of the Swanage Regatta and Carnival Organisation. She would stay with her daughters at the Grosvenor Hotel and indulged her passion for golf on the Isle of Purbeck course.

Bollards or cannon-bollards - actual cannon were used on street corners and other busy places in the City of London [from the 1750s] to keep wagons on the carriageway and prevent them damaging the footway.

There were plenty of cracked, captured or obsolete cannon during the Napoleonic wars [1793-1815] but the supply was soon outstripped by demand.

Foundries in London and Staffordshire began making cast-iron imitation cannon, smaller than the real thing, without trunnions and with raised rings so that horses could be tethered just below the rounded tops. At the other end, intended for below ground, the round cross-sections became square as this tended to be more stable. As with cannon, insignia and lettering could also be added to the replica made by the pattern-maker which then went into the foundry sand-boxes to make the mould for the molten iron.

Designs quickly developed, away from the simple but elegant copy of a cannon, and each London parish wanted its bollards to look different from those of the surrounding areas. The round pattern evolved into square and even octagonal and hexagonal shapes, often further refined with bevels and flutings.

When Purbeck contractors John Mowlem and George Burt started laying proper raised, kerbed pavements through the streets of London [from 1823] many bollards became redundant. By the 1880s, Burt was shipping them to Swanage - he must have brought a couple of hundred, given that 111 survivors were counted in 1973.

Many were drilled with holes and had hinge-pins fitted by a blacksmith so that they were usable as gateposts, which aided their dispersal into the new suburbs and even the lanes and fields. One or two were de-capped and fitted with tubing to convert them into gas lamps.

They are a more representative collection than you will find in a similar walking distance anywhere in London, and include some parish names that are hardly ever mentioned today:

> ST ANNE'S & ST GILES
> ST ANNE'S SOHO
> SAINT GEORGE HANOVER SQUARE
> ST MARTIN-IN-THE-FIELDS
> ST JAMES CLERKENWELL
> ST JAMES WESTMINSTER
> CHRIST CHURCH MIDDLESEX

CITY OF LONDON
CITY OF WESTMINSTER

Emblems include the coats-of-arms of the cities of London and Westminster and a crown and "IV WR" for "4 William Rex" - King William the fourth [reigned 1830-37].

Boundary stones - the parish line between Swanage and Studland runs for more than a mile along the hog's back spine of Ballard Down, from the slopes of the Ulwell Gap in the west to exposed chalk of Ballard Cliff in the east, where it drops southwards and seaward to yield Ballard Point or Head to Studland.

This is now a fence-line, with National Trust land on each side, but it was traditionally unhedged and a former open sheep-leaze. The length of the boundary along the summit, a distance of 2,050 yards, was marked in the eighteenth century by eight marker stones which are cut on the south-facing side with "S M" for Swanage Manor.

The penultimate stone from the east, 250 yards west from the main cluster of Bronze Age round barrows (Ordnance Survey map reference SZ 038 813), is dated 1776. Swanage public bridleway number 6 follows the south side of this boundary and passes all the stones (from SZ 021 813 in the west to SZ 040 813 in the east).

Brewery - see entry for **Swanage Pale Ale**

Brickyard Lane, at Ulwell - see entry for **Swanage Brick Works**

Brodick Castle - Paisley-built [1878], this double-funnel paddle-steamer was bought by the Bournemouth, Swanage and Poole Steam Packet Company [1887] to replace their previous flagship *Bournemouth* which lay as a wreck on the rocks of Portland Bill [July 1886].

Her replacement was then acquired by Cosens and Company of Weymouth [1901] and would be sold on retirement [1909] for use as an Argentinian cattle-barge. Ironically she failed to sail beyond sight of her predecessor's grave, taking water and sinking whilst being towed round Portland Bill [1910] on the first leg of what should have been her transatlantic voyage [1910].

The Brook - otherwise unnamed, being the stream that comes into Swanage from Harman's Cross, midway to Corfe Castle, and which used to become tidal at Herston. Thereafter it was effectively the Backwater [see its entry]. The only crossing point was below St Mary's Church, to Northbrook Road. Here, beside Swanwic House, is now the only section of the Brook that has not been put into a culvert.

It is concealed under the shops along the north side of Station Road and had its revenge in 1914 and again in November 1935 when floodwater brought boats back to the streets. Severe floods recurred later in the century, notably on 3 February 1990. The brook flows, or overflows, into the bay immediately to the south of the Mowlem Theatre.

Freshwater joins it from springs at Frogwell, near the Town Hall, and Springfield, which supplied Panton's brewery [closed 1893]. Another bubbles directly into the sea across Monkey Beach, near the old Stone Jetty, and was the place where boatmen replenished their water supplies.

Extensive work has been carried out [1992-93] to provide Victoria Avenue with a culvert to take storm-water out to sea. This outfall runs through a large raised extension to the beach at the bottom of The Avenue.

Bullen - for **Lady Bullen** see entry for **Newton Cottage**

Tom Burnham's Oak - marks the site of a suicide burial, probably with a stake through his heart to lay the ghost, which took place as custom dictated: beside the highway, at what was then a crossroads on the parish boundary (Ordnance Survey map reference SZ 010 800). He was from Langton Matravers and is buried beneath an oak tree at an old road junction near Godlingston, at the boundary between Langton Matravers and Swanage. Burnham had hanged himself. Despite the unmarked grave, his name, at least, has persisted with the tree named Tom Burnham's Oak, standing beside Burnham's Lane.

There are two junctions in Burnham's Lane and in 1961 George Clark of 34 Steer Road, Swanage, clarified the position of Burnham's Oak as being that on the parish boundary, which was the traditional location for suicide burials:

"I attended Herston School fifty years ago and the lanes and fields close by were our playgrounds. The particular oak is quite fifty yards from the crossroad. The tree bore the deeply cut initials T.B. for Tom Burnham. The limb on which he tied the rope had long since been sawn off as was the usual custom. A story rife at that time was that Tom was buried under the green mound at the crossroad, but some said it was the burial place of a witch, a wooden stake having been driven through her body. Whilst on the subject of burials outside consecrated ground a few years ago a skeleton was dug up in a quarry at Langton. It was only four feet below the surface. At an inquiry it was held to be the remains of a coloured man, no doubt washed ashore nearby. Presumably a colour bar operated in those days and he was not deemed a fit subject to be buried in the local church."

A later instance of a suicide's burial - after 1823 when the law had banned stakings or other mutilation - was that of John Ball, landlord of the old Ship Inn at Langton Matravers. This building is now a cottage nestling beside the three-storey inn which replaced it on the summit of Steps Hill in 1884. R.J. Saville documented John Ball's case in issue 17 of Dorset County Magazine.

John Ball had parted from his wife, Mary Holmes Ball. On the night of 18 December 1878 they came together again for Christmas. After closing-time they had their last row. Mary ran back to her mother's home and John followed with a shotgun. She was barely behind the cottage door as it was hit by a blast of shot. John went back to the inn and shot himself in the public room.

Rev Lester Lester, rector of Langton, wrote to a local newspaper:
"The body of John Ball, late of the Ship Inn, Langton, was buried like a dog at 9.30 p.m. on 22 December. For charity's sake we must protest against this! It is time for even Purbeck juries to know that the sentiment of our times is dead against such verdicts as *felo-de-se*. He wanted his wife to come and live with him. She felt that she could not. Life then appeared so black to him that he shot himself. If he was sane, why be so cruel to survivors, so uncourteous to a poor dead man; seeing that to him prayers could mean nothing, and even a suicide's burial nothing, while to them the touching service might have been of vital importance. We do hope that verdict will be the last of its kind in our neighbourhood."

He started a letter writing campaign against *felo-de-se* ('felon of himself'). This was "the crime of suicide" and it was society's retribution on the body of the deceased, The rector's letters supported a winning cause as the law was repealed by Parliament in Acts of 1880 and 1882. Suicides were afterwards buried in a churchyard as if they had died normally.

Burt - Victorian entrepreneur and developer **George Burt** [1816-94] was described as "the King of Swanage" by Thomas Hardy.

Boss of Swanage stone trade, he edged its operations out of the town. He started the first steamer service from the pier and began to transform the old stone port into a seaside spa. By the 1880s he was building and selling houses on a scale that turned Swanage into the fastest expanding town of its size in Dorset.

He rebuilt Purbeck House in the High Street [1875] and brought home numerous pieces of old London to embellish not only it but the town generally and the surrounding countryside as well. Burt was the nephew and business associate of wealthy contractor John Mowlem.

The novelist Thomas Hardy wrote that Burt was rougher in speech than he would have expected after his years in London "being the ordinary type of Dorsetman, self-made by trade, whenever one of the county does self-make himself, which is not often".

Burt - heir apparent **Sir John Mowlem Burt** [1845-1918], son of George Burt and great nephew of John Mowlem, propelled the contracting dynasty of John Mowlem & Co Ltd into royal commissions. He was knighted for his refurbishment of Westminster Abbey for Edward VII's coronation [1902].

Burt - stone merchant **Robert Burt** [1788-1847], father of George, lived at 1 Victoria Terrace, Swanage, and has an elaborate fluted column above his grave in the old parish churchyard, south-east of St Mary's.

In 1812 he married Laetitia (Lettie) Manwell [1786-1851] and their children were George [1816], Elizabeth [1818], Robert [1821], Charles [1823], Francis [1825] and Susannah [1829].

California Farm - Swanage's most far-flung farmstead, formerly known as Herston Farm and lying on the southern edge of the quarries in the coastal hinterland midway between Herston and Round Down (Ordnance Survey map reference SZ 020 777).

Given that it lies a mile south-west of the town, beyond the quarrylands, and could only be reached by an indirect stony track from Herston, it must have gained its name from its inaccessibility. A literal translation of California is unlikely, in that it comes from the Spanish for "hot furnace," an allusion to the climate.

It is a late eighteenth century building with a nineteenth century porch.

Cannon-ball column - this seafront granite monument was raised by John Mowlem [1862] to give Swanage a little history. It commemorates an alleged battle between the Saxons and the Danes in Swanage Bay. Sir Frederick Treves started the laugh about it in 1906 when he wrote *Highways and Byways in Dorset*:

"Amongst other litter in the London contractor's yard there would seem to have been some cannon balls. The faithful pavior [a stone paver] evidently had some difficulty in working these in for the adornment of his birthplace. Cannon balls suggest battle, but there has been no battle at Swanage. King Alfred, however, is supposed to have defeated the Danes in Swanage Bay in the year of our Lord 877. Naturally enough, the contractor erected a pillar on the Marine Parade to commemorate this proud if dim event, and placed the cannon balls on top of it. To some these missiles may appear inappropriate, as gunpowder was not invented until more than 400 years after the assumed engagement."

Professor F.M. Stenton in his *Anglo-Saxon England* does not consider there was a battle at all but says that a Danish fleet, bringing reinforcements to raiders attacking Exeter, "was destroyed by a storm off Swanage". One hundred and twenty ships were lost, the Anglo Saxon Chronicle records. A dramatic account of the loss was incorporated in *The Namesake* by C. Walter Hodges.

The debate on history and the monument resumed at Swanage urban council's meeting in October 1965 when A.E.R. Gray said the monument was an object of general ridicule. The claim that it commemorated a battle against the Danes in Swanage Bay was historically inaccurate and the three cannon balls surmounting it were likened to a pawnbroker's sign. He said: "The day of monuments has passed. This one should be demolished and sunk to the bottom of the bay."

The discussion concerned the re-siting of the column which stood in the way of development on the promenade. Members decided to spend £200 on moving it, rather than £75 for demolition. So the monument, erected in 1862, still stands though without one of its original four cannon balls. This fell off many years ago and was later washed up near Old Harry Rocks.

The only genuine history is in the three remaining cannon balls. These were unexploded thirteen-inch Russian shells brought back to Portsmouth in the sides of wooden battleships that had fought the Crimean War in the Black Sea and the Baltic.

Cannon-bollards - see entry for **Bollards**

Cemeteries - the parish's first detached cemetery, immediately across the road from St Mary's Church, was consecrated on 12 October 1826. Its now wooded slope overlooks the south-east corner of the church and some of the stones, including that of its founder, rector Rev Thomas Oldfeld Bartlett, have been displaced for seats to make it look like a park, and more user-friendly for those who leave Coke cans.

Memorials survive mainly at the top end, including the "ROBERT BURT FAMILY VAULT".

The second Victorian cemetery, a town one rather than an Anglican preserve, covers 1½ acres [opened 1856] on the other side of the Brook and the Railway on the west-side of the south end of Northbrook Road (Ordnance Survey map reference SZ 027 790). It is a place of quietude and tranquillity, marred only by the fact that it now has to contend with the bland architecture of Gilbert Court; inmates there are luckier in the view from their windows than any hapless dead looking up from amongst the headstones.

Gilbert Court even overshadows the one great tomb, that of John Mowlem which rises sheer and then stepped to be surmounted by a pyramid of matching blue Guernsey granite - 20 feet above the grass - as the topmost piece of the cemetery. Dwarfing all else - until Gilbert Court.

The much more extensive twentieth century Swanage Cemetery, initially covering 7 acres [opened 1931] is in open countryside at Washpond Lane, Godlingston, in a pleasant location beneath the Purbeck Hills (SZ 019 801). It has since been expanded across more ex-Bankes Estate land. There is a little chapel but it is architecturally undistinguished.

Charlotte Mary - the town's first lifeboat, launched in 1875 [*see entry for 'Lifeboat'*].

Chinchen - despite sounding Chinese, this was and is a good old Swanage name, as is shown by the stone to Nathan Chinchen in St Mary's Church. It expounds Victorian confidence in the certainty of life extending to whatever might happen after death, with its record of "a name well-known in this vicinity in his generation". He died in his 85th year, on 16 May 1840: "His beloved remains are deposited in a vault in the burying ground adjacent, where he was placed in the sure and certain hope that when those that sleep in the dust of the earth shall awake, he will rise clothed in his redeemer's righteousness to everlasting life."

There are many more stones like that, including the epitaph of an anonymous 22-year-old in 1844: "My affliction is blest tis the work of my God. O merciful Father I welcome the rod, since by it I am brought to a sense of my sin. Ere I go to the grave where none pardon can win ..."

Chinchen - prisoner of the Japanese **Henry James Chinchen** died in Sandakan Camp, North Borneo, on 14 April 1943. He was the 29-year-old son of Harry and Frances Chinchen. They are buried in Swanage Cemetery, Washpond Lane, Godlingston.

The Clock Tower - a magnificent edifice of Victorian gothic, now clockless, standing at Rockleigh between the Pier and Lifeboat Station on the northern side of the Peveril Point promontory (Ordnance Survey map reference SZ 037 786). Designed as a memorial to the first Duke of Wellington [1769-1852], it was erected at the Southwark end of London Bridge [1854]. The clock, which had transparent dials, was made for the Great Exhibition [1851], though in the tower it was a constant disappointment with the vibrations of London's passing traffic making it a poor time-keeper.

The principal view of the Clock Tower was then blocked by the building of a railway viaduct on the south side of Duke Street Hill [1863], towards Waterloo East, Hungerford Bridge and into Charing Cross. The Metropolitan Police called it "an unwarrantable obstruction" and the structure was demolished [1866].

London contractor and Swanage quarry owner George Burt had it shipped to Swanage and re-erected towards the south-east corner of Swanage Bay. Until 1904 it had an attractive spire but a religious fanatic objected and insisted it was replaced by a cupola. As for the clock, it never reached Swanage, so you can see through its circular opening to the sky, indeed the stars for a deeper perception of time.

Cluny Red Cross Hospital - during the Great War, Dorset 36 Voluntary Aid Detachment ran the hospital at Cluny, in Cluny Crescent (postcode BH19 2BS), on the southern slopes of the town. The large house was loaned by the trustees of Kenneth Anderson. It was opened as a hospital on 9 November 1914 and closed on 15 January 1919.

With 50 beds it initially treated the sick and wounded from the tented camp established at Swanage for Kitchener's army, receiving 231 patients by the end of 1914. In 1915 the number rose to 851 admissions, but then [November 1915] the camp's own hospital was opened and Cluny's 318 cases in 1916 were mainly from overseas, transferred for recuperation from Christchurch Hospital or Cornelia Hospital, Poole. The numbers were 311 for 1917 and 272 for 1918.

Because critical and surgical cases were not generally admitted the death rate was consequently low, totalling only three and all those in 1915 - two of cerebral meningitis and one with pneumonia.

The hospital was usually quite full: "Under the able Matronship of Sister Henry, the Hospital gained a great reputation with Tommy as a happy place, where he was well fed, comfortably housed, and his medicine and surgical needs carefully attended to.

"Discipline was well maintained, and the advantage of this was felt when in 1918 a fire broke out at the hospital, and was only prevented from becoming very serious, by the prompt action of Orderly Hibbs, aided by the patients, who fought the flames successfully."

A.J.B. Unwin acted as its honorary secretary.

On demobilization, stores valued at £127 5s 6d were donated to the Cottage Hospital in Swanage [May 1919].

Collins - solicitor **Sir Geoffrey Abdy Collins** [1888-1982] was a member of the council of the Law Society [1931-56] and knighted during his term as its president [1951-52]. He lived at Mullion, 20 Ballard Estate, Swanage.

Congregational Chapel - see entry for **United Reform Church**

Conservative Club - 27 Kings Road, Swanage (postcode BH19 1HE) built by the third Earl of Eldon [1911] to replace the previous premises, Mimilake on the other side of the street at 28 Kings Road East.

Constitution - nearly a wreck on shingle between Ballard Point and Old Harry Rocks "in the haze and mist of the night" on 17 January 1879. "The boom of guns quickly made known the fact" as the United States frigate announced her plight.

She was homeward bound from France with products for the Paris Exhibition on the American side of the Atlantic.

Guns, chains, cable and other heavy items were removed to lighten the old three-masted sailing vessel in the morning. Five steamers then spent several hours trying to pull her clear. Eventually a government tug arrived, from Southampton, and this additional assistance enabled them to release the *Constitution*. She was towed to Portsmouth, where only minor damage was found, and resumed her transatlantic voyage.

Convent of Our Lady of Mercy - see entry for **Purbeck House**

Coventry - colonial soldier **Captain Frederick Coventry** [?1820-46] of the Grove, Swanage, and the 29th Regiment, has a memorial in St Mary's Church: "The life of this most amiable and promising young officer was spared in the battle field at Sobraon [against the Sikhs, 10 February 1846] but he fell victim to the climate of India on the 29th of July 1846 in the

26th year of his age. His remains lie deposited in the burial ground at Kussowlie."

Cuckoo Pound - Purbeck traditionally receives the first cuckoos in the county, often in the first week of April and dependably in time for Wareham Spring Fair [formerly 17 April] where, it was said "he buys himself a pair of breeches". Most parishes in south-east Dorset have their Cuckoo Pen or Cuckoo Pound, attaching to small and often wooded enclosures.

These date to the eighteenth century or earlier and usually seem to be close to former areas of extensive common grazing rights. There is one south of Verney Farm, a hundred yards west of the Swanage boundary and in the parish of Langton Matravers. This small wood - interestingly the only trees on the central stone plateau of southern Purbeck - lies midway between South Farm and Blackers Hole, half a mile from the sea (Ordnance Survey map reference SZ 008 776).

It was a common belief, before and indeed after Gilbert White's time, that cuckoos, like swallows, hibernated in hollow trees. Logically, always a perilous thing to bring to folklore, they were first heard in the Cuckoo Pounds and therefore believed to have over-wintered there.

Another bit of the reasoning, is that before falling into disuse and becoming overgrown, these enclosures had their origin as stock pounds for bullocks and hogs being gathered for the Cuckoo Fair, as it was called, at Wareham. Cuckoo Fair Pounds became Cuckoo Pounds as fairgoing declined. The bird's association with the event came about because it is the reliable audible clock for the first couple of weeks in April.

Danish fleet, wrecked off Swanage in 877 - the earliest recorded Purbeck shipwrecks changed the course of English history. In 876, following months of fighting, the West Saxons bribed the Danes, who had sailed into Wareham, to negotiate a truce. Saxon money was exchanged for the return of hostages and the Danes also gave King Alfred their solemn oath "on the holy ring" to leave Wessex. The enemy departed from Wareham but occupied Exeter instead.

The *Anglo-Saxon Chronicle* is ambiguous about the sequence and nature of events. The decisive moment was either gale-force winds or fog off Purbeck in 877 when ships were making for Exeter - perhaps reinforcements rather than the original force from Wareham as implied by the *Chronicle*. Three versions of the manuscript say they "encountered a great storm at sea, and 120 ships were lost at Swanage"; the other two versions have it that they "encountered a great mist at sea, and 120 ships were lost at Swanage". In all probability it was a combination of foul weather, with disorientation in thick fog being followed by the gale. The failure of the full Danish force to reach Exeter caused the remainder to accede to Alfred's demands and quit the city, leaving for Gloucester which was in Mercian territory.

Delamotte - this medical family's memorials on the wall of St Mary's Church include **Henry Digby Cotes Delamotte** [1796-1874] "for over fifty years a surgeon of this town" and **George Cotes Delamotte** [1829-1922] of Osborne House, "who for many years was a medical practitioner of this town and was churchwarden of this parish for 17 years".

Dinosaur *Dorsetochelys delairi* - in the mid-1970s science caught up with a fossil which had lain in Dorset County Museum since 1908. It came from the Purbeck Beds at Swanage and only the upper part of a turtle skull was visible as the rest of the animal was embedded in stone. Rather than risk damaging it, the skull was left in the lump of limestone.

Using an acetic acid solution technicians at the Zoology Museum in Cambridge dissolved away the matrix of encrustation. This released the skull and its intricate lower side could be examined for the first time.

It was only the second turtle skull known from the Isle of Purbeck and the scientists found they were dealing with not only a new species but a new genus as well. It shares features with two other turtle families and is thought to be an evolutionary link between them.

The animal was alive one hundred million years ago when southern England was covered by tropical swampland on the edge of a warm sea. The skull has been called *Dorsetochelys delairi*, its specific name a tribute to the work of Purbeck fossil reptile collector Justin Delair. The skull is on display in the County Museum in Dorchester.

Dinosaur *Purbeckopus pentactylus* - Purbeck continues to produce more dinosaur footprints than any other area in the British Isles; in fact probably more than everywhere else added together. The major find of modern times was on the edge of the nineteenth century Townsend Quarries, on the southern side of Swanage, beneath the building plot that has become number 19 Townsend Road. Builder David Selby cracked open a stone and found a distinct three-toed dinosaur footprint.

It was in the Laning vein of the Purbeck Beds, and Paul Ensom of the Dorset County Museum led an excavation in August 1981 which revealed large hollows, pushed into the stone, indicating that the dinosaur had lain down in what was then mud. The reptile is usually identified as the megalosaurus, though sometimes the traces are from previously unknown species, with *Purbeckopus pentactylus* being named after a unique set of six-inch prints which was found in a quarry to the west of the quarrying hamlet of Acton.

One long length of prints, more than seventy feet of them, was dug out from E.W. Suttle's Mutton Hole Quarry at Herston and is now displayed in the forecourt of the British Museum of Natural History in Kensington.

Dog-carts - regarded as something of an anachronism in the first phase of Victorian England, a vivid account of this form of canine transportation comes from Swanage. Here they were used by marine store dealers who came with china and other goods and left with iron, rags and bones. These dealers had dog-carts, about three feet long, two feet wide and a foot deep, hauled by two or three bulldogs. William Masters Hardy remembered:

"I have seen the carts overloaded and the dogs compelled to claw themselves uphill, with mouths wide open, tongues hanging out, panting like harts in the chase, and bodies nearly touching the ground."

Those dogs were British bulldogs of the old breed, fine specimens of the days before the animals were deformed according to the rules of breeding that have produced the present hideous malfunctioning creatures which carry a pedigree and win praise at shows. Today's fat, debased bulldogs would die under the strain of a dogcart and are lucky that Parliament outlawed the things in 1854.

Durlston blow-hole - as with the Thurlestone in Devon and the Durdle Door at Lulworth (*th* was replaced by *d* in the Dorset dialect) the name Durlston means "pierced rock". There was a blow-hole on the headland, drawn by Philip Brannon about 1860 and possibly blocked by falling debris when Durlston Castle was built. It spouted with the waves.

A.D. Mills, in *The Place-Names of Dorset*, agrees that although there are quarry tunnels at Durlston "the name no doubt refers to some earlier natural coastal feature". I have two copies of the Brannon engraving in which it occurs, in my collection, but I have not noticed any mentions of the holed-stone. The print shows a spurt of water which after allowing for perspective is rising half-way up the cliff, that is about twenty-five feet above sea level. It is captioned: "The Blow Hole Transverse faults and contorted beds, Durlston Head."

Durlston Castle - George Burt's major monument on Durlston Head is the corbel-turreted restaurant, set on the cliffs and surrounded by innumerable tablets of stone inscribed with statistics and poetry. It is a palatial French riviera-style villa of Purbeck stone, built in 1886-87 on land George Burt had bought in 1864.

Three granite pillars were ordered by Sir Charles Barry for Trafalgar Square but turned out to be surplus to requirements and were inscribed by Burt: "Durlston Head Castle, above sea 215 feet." Its sundial, on the south wall, is dated 1887.

At the end of the headland is another of Burt's information stones: "Above sea 111ft."

Durlston Country Park - cliffs south of Swanage were selected in the early 1970s for Dorset's first country park and a significant holding of council land, already highly popular with visitors, was expanded by leasing adjoining fields. This was a Victorian and Edwardian playground and overflows with the history of seaside tourism as well as important wildlife habitats.

In 1974 Durlston Country Park was opened. County planning officer Alan Swindall explained that the management plan had been designed to preserve "the rich ecological pattern" by a "careful balance between people and nature". It includes some of the last sea-cliff nesting sites of the auks, and concentrations of orchids across Round Down. The park incorporates Durlston Head, Anvil Point and a subterranean access problem in the form of Tilly Whim Caves which were closed through fear of accidents. Inland the park extends half-a-mile, to within one field of California Farm, Durlston Farm and South Barn. On the western edge it joins the National Trust's Belle Vue holding.

The long-running friction between naturalists and climbers has been smoothed by a compromise that creates sanctuaries and areas with a closed season, but allows unrestricted access elsewhere.

Some of the climbs rank amongst the most popular in the country and the classic ones have their own names, including Rendezvous Manque between Durlston Head and Tilly Whim Caves, and Traverse of the Gods between the caves and the lighthouse. At the side of the headland is the Subliminal Cliff. Westwards from Anvil Point are Via Christina, Nutcracker Exit, Marmolata Buttress, Sheerline, Bottomless Buttress and Boulder Ruckle Exit.

Durlston's first marsupials - 65 million years ago the first small shrew-like mammals were given an opportunity to occupy niches from which the ubiquitous dinosaurs had been removed. These prototype mammals were helped by their small size to pull through the disaster. After the catastrophe, mammals ruled the world and no traces of dinosaurs are found in later rocks.

Yet neither are there any fossils to explain the sequence of intermediaries between the reptiles and their successors, the mammals. Clearly, the mammals did not come about through gradual evolution, but erupted suddenly as a result of some dramatic interruption to the order of the world.

That Purbeck holds the clues to the truth is apparent from the reptilian evidence in the quarrylands and also from the fact that one of the earliest mammal beds in the country is on the cliffs at Durlston Bay where scattered remains of marsupials have been found. They show the start of the advanced stages of mammal development that have led to ourselves; though not what created the marsupials.

Durlston Inscriptions - these, around George Burt's Durlston Castle [*see its entry and that for the Globe*] date from 1887-91 and are a marvellous pot-pourri of late Victorian outlook and scientific knowledge. Where else can you be reminded in tablets of stone that the longest day in Spitzbergen lasts 3½ months and that a ship on the horizon at sea level will have lost 66 feet 4 inches of its visual superstructure at 10 miles? Therefore I shall reproduce them in what appears to be their entirety:

An iron coast and angry waves,
You seem to hear them rise and fall,
And roar rock thwarted in their bellowing caves,
Beneath the windy wall.

Let Prudence direct you, Temperance chasten you,
Fortitude support you;
And Justice be the Guide to all your actions.
All are but parts of one stupendous whole,
Whose body Nature is, and God the soul;
Look round our World, behold the chain of Love
Combining all below and all above.
See plastic Nature working to this end,
The single atoms each to other tend,
All serv'd, all serving, nothing stands alone,
The chain holds on, and where it ends unknown.
Pope

God, the Creator, and Ruler of the Universe.

By the Way of the Lord were the Heavens made.
And all the host of them by the Breath of His mouth,
For He spake and it was done,
He commanded and it stood fast.

Psalm xxxiii, 6-9.

When I consider Thy Heavens, the Moon and the Stars which Thou hast ordained, What is man that Thou are mindful of Him?

Psalm viii, 3-4.

Our Nature consists in motion, perfect rest is Death.

Pascal.

DURATION OF LONGEST DAY

at

| London | 16 hours 30 mins. | Spitzbergen | 3½ months. |
| Hamburg | 19 hours 0 mins. | The Poles | 6 months. |

CLOCK TIMES OF THE WORLD

These differ from Greenwich, 4 minutes every degree.

When 12 o'clock noon at Greenwich it is:-

EAST at WEST

Paris	...	12.09 p.m.	Swanage	...	11.52 a.m.
Rome	...	12.50 p.m.	Edinburgh	...	11.47 a.m.
Vienna	...	1.06 p.m.	Dublin	...	11.35 a.m.
Calcutta	...	5.54 p.m.	New York	...	7.04 a.m.

CONVEXITY OF THE OCEAN

On looking at a vessel from ocean level we lose,

if one mile distant	0ft. 8ins.
five miles distant	16ft. 7ins.
ten miles distant	66ft. 4ins.

The Seas but join the nations they divide.

TIDES

These are caused by the attraction of the sun and moon. The rise and fall of water being much influenced by local conditions. Rise of tides at:

	Spring	Neap
Bristol Channel	38ft. 0in.	29ft. 0in.
Jersey ...	31ft. 6in.	23ft. 0in.
Southampton	13ft. 0in.	9ft. 6in.
Swanage ...	6ft. 0in.	4ft. 0in.
Wexford ...	5ft. 0in.	3ft. 6in.

THE EARTH

The Earth is a Planet, and one of God's glorious creations, shewing the wonders of land, air, and sea. As seen from the nearest planet it would appear like the beautiful "Evening Star," having its place in the mighty system of worlds, as a part of the marvellous plan of the universe.

Equatorial Diameter about ... 7,926 miles.

Equatorial Circumference about ... 24,900 miles.

The Surface consists of about three parts water and one part land.

Revolves on its axis from west to east once in 23 hours, 56 minutes, 4 seconds, and moves round the Sun once in 365 days, 5 hours, 48 minutes, 48 seconds.

The rate of the Earth's motion at the Equator is about 1,040 miles per hour.

A Gale of Wind travels at the rate of 80 to 100 miles per hour

The Common Black Swift flies at the rate of 200 miles per hour

The Swallow flies at the rate of 100 miles per hour

The Carrier Pigeon flies at the rate of 40 miles per hour

The Earth is one of a family of eight large planets, revolving round the Sun in nearly circular paths, and depending upon him for their light and heat.

The Sun rotates once in 25¼ days, to a point on the Solar Equator, and is whirled round with a velocity of 4,500 miles per hour.

THE SUN

The largest of the Heavenly bodies comprised within the Solar System, has a diameter of about 862,000 miles, and is the source of light and heat.

Mean distance from the Earth approx. 92,000,000 miles.

Crosses the Equator twice in the year, viz., at the vernal equinox (March 21st) and at the autumnal equinox (September 21st), causing the varying seasons on Earth.

THE MOON

Diameter about one-fourth that of the Earth, 2,160 miles.

Mean distance from the Earth, about 238,800 miles.

Moves round the Earth once in a lunar month (28 days), and revolves on her axis once in the same time. Hence, very nearly the same portion of the Moon's surface is always turned towards the Earth. The attraction of the Sun and Moon on the Earth produces the phenomena of the Tides, that of the Moon being about three times as great as that of the Sun.

"Give me the ways of wandering stars to know,
The depths of Heaven above and earth below,
Teach me the various labours of the moon,
And whence proceed the eclipses of the sun;
Why flowing tides prevail upon the main;
And in what dark recess they shrink again;
What shakes the solid earth, what cause delays
The summer nights, and shortens winter days."

Virgil, 70-19 B.C.

(Translated by John Dryden, 1631-1700)

THE STARS

The distance from the Earth of the nearest fixed star, "Alpha Centauri," visible in the Southern Hemisphere, is computed to be 200,000 times that of the Sun. Light, which travels at the rate of about 186,000 miles in a second, would be three-and-a-half years in reaching the Earth from this Star.

> This World was once a fluid haze of light,
> Till toward the centre set the starry tides,
> And Eddied into suns, that wheeling cast
> The Planets.
> *Tennyson.*

O Thou Eternal One! Whose Presence bright
All space doth occupy - all motion guide;
Thou from primeval nothingness didst call,
First chaos, then existence. Lord on thee
Eternity has its foundation! All
Spring forth from Thee! All light, joy, harmony!
Sole origin! All life, all beauty, Thine!
Thy Word created all, and doth create!
Thy splendour fills all space with rays divine!
Thou art, and wert, and shall be! Glorious! Great
Life-Giving, life-sustaining Potentate!
(Dershavin, 1743-1816)

I made Him just and right.
Sufficient to have stood, though free to fall.
Milton.

Let Nature be your teacher.   *Wordsworth.*

SWANAGE ENCYCLOPAEDIC GUIDE 34

Accuse not Nature! She hath done her part
Do thou but thine! *Milton.*

One touch of Nature makes the whole world kin.
Shakespeare.

Comparative sizes (on the same scale as this Globe, [see its entry], which is ten feet in diameter), mean diameters, and least and greatest distances in miles from the Earth of the Sun, Moon and Planets. The Globe stands 136 feet above sea level.

	Comparative sizes		Mean diameter	Least	Greatest
	Feet	Inches	in miles	Distance	Distance
The Sun would be	1090	0	866,400	89,900,000	93,000,000
Jupiter	109	0	86,500	409,000,000	592,000,000
Saturn	92	0	73,000	831,000,000	1,015,000,000
Neptune	44	0	34,800	2,629,000,000	2,863,000,000
Uranus	40	0	31,900	1,746,000,000	1,929,000,000
The Earth	10	0	7,918	-	-
Venus	9	3	7,700	24,000,000	159,550,000
Mars	5	4	4,200	36,000,000	245,000,000
Mercury	4	0	3,000	47,000,000	136,000,000
The Moon	2	9	2,160	221,600	253,000

Notice, to the left of the exit, a large scratched slab with these words carved at the top: "Persons wishing to write their names will please do so on this stone only."

Some have taken up the offer and the tablets generally have not been subjected to graffiti.

The path westward has its own inscription:

"An iron coast and angry waves
You seem to hear them rise and fall.
And roar rock - thwarted in their bellowing caves
Beneath the windy wall.
Above sea 149 ft."

Durlston Model Railway - shipping magnate Sir Edward Nicholl [1862-1939] of Littleton Park, Shepperton, never forgot his humble but stimulating beginnings as an apprentice engineer on the Great Western Railway. In fact he went on to romanticise it on the grand scale, if of necessity in miniature, as the archetypal "Model Electric Railway" with 500 feet of track at 2-inches gauge, accompanied all down the line with realistic scenery, villages, towns, an aerodrome and Brunel-designed viaducts, bridges and tunnels.

Ostensibly for the benefit of his grandchildren, it was removed from the conservatory of his mansion - which became Shepperton Studios, the Sound City of the film moguls - and brought to Durlston Castle.

"Everyone cannot but be interested in the unique collection of models which make the railway probably the most comprehensive display in this country," to quote its 1954 brochure.

Edmonds - naval hero **Joseph Edmonds** [1720-94] retired to Swanage. His monument, above the vestry door in St Mary's Church, shows two ships engaged in battle: "Commander of the *Defiance* of 24 guns whose bravery in conquering a French ship of superior force in 1758 was generously rewarded by the underwriters and merchants of the City of London."

He died at Swanage on 26 September 1794 at the age of 74, perhaps when news reached England of the death of his eldest son, James, in Jamaica on 5 July 1794. James, aged 33, was in command of the *New Albion*.

The year of tragedy was to continue for Joseph's widow, Priscilla, with the death of their youngest son, 29-year-old John, commander of the

Dorset "who was kill'd gallantly defending his ship against the French off the island of Cuba 21st October 1794". Priscilla Edmonds survived them, and died on 18 March 1801 at the age of 75.

Edward's walking tour - the formal education of Prince Edward [1841-1910], Queen Victoria's eldest son, included walking tours, the first of which he set out on in 1856 at the age of fifteen. The Dorset and Devon countryside was chosen. Edward - Bertie to his friends, and later King Edward VII - left Osborne in the Isle of Wight towards the end of September, travelling incognito with two male aides, one in his thirties and the other in middle age. They saw Sandbanks and were ferried to Brownsea Island and then went inland to visit Wimborne Minster.

On 26 September they arrived in Swanage and booked into the Royal Victoria Hotel for the night. The landlord said he could only accommodate the two men and "the young gentleman must put up with a sofa in the corridor". A suitable word in the man's ear avoided that fate but from here the disguise was eroded and soon an expectancy gripped the countryside. Though they set out from Swanage along the cliff-path to St Alban's Head the following stage was in their carriage. It included stops at Wareham and Dorchester, where the prince was recognised at a service in St Peter's Church. The tour was broken off at Honiton because of increasing popular interest.

Edward, Prince of Wales, forced down at Godlingston - Purbecks's least expected royal visit took place about 1.15 in the afternoon, on 12 July 1933 when the Prince of Wales [1894-1972, briefly King Edward VIII] landed in a cornfield near Godlingston Farm. The Channel coast was being lashed by a gale and the Prince, after flying over Bournemouth, was heading for Weymouth, to open the harbour and pier reconstruction.

Visibility was becoming poor and the plane increasingly bumped by the wind. Prince Edward asked the pilot to land in a field. He took his position from the buildings of Swanage Brick and Tile Company, using the chimney stack as a landmark and circling it a couple of times as he descended.

"We thought at first he was going to knock if off," said works director B.P. Codling, referring to the chimney, "but the plane came down nicely in a little wheatfield on the other side of the road from here, on land owned by the Bankes Estate [now National Trust property]. The pilot pulled her up by the side of a rick. Afterwards we could find no trace of its descent, the wheat being quite undamaged. Several of our tilers who were near rushed to the assistance of the plane, having seen it in the air, and got the impression it was in difficulties."

The pilot admitted the landing had been far from easy. As for Prince Edward, he was given a lift to Weymouth by Captain F.R. Bacon of the brickworks. Britain's most fashionable dapper-dresser arrived looking none too spruce, the Bournemouth Daily Echo reported: "His hair was very ruffled and his suede shoes were clogged with mud. His trouser ends were bespattered with mud."

Emmanuel Baptist Church - brick-built on the south side of the High Street, beside the corner with Howard Road (Ordnance Survey map reference SZ 023 788).

Foundation stones were laid by Beatrice Ellen Beebe and Pastor James Wicks on 19 June 1920. Above, over the door, another tablet of Purbeck stone proclaims: "To the glory of God this Chapel was erected and opened free of debt in answer to prayer. May 1921."

Empress - Thames-built [1879] and owned by Cosens and Company of Weymouth, this single-funnel oscillating engine vessel would have the longest career of all the paddle-steamers in local waters [1880-1955].

Her end was conventional, in the breaker's yard, but there are still distinguished titbits with her engine - the last of its type - being preserved in Southampton Maritime Museum, and the boat appears in David Lean's classic film of Charles Dickens's *Great Expectations* [1946].

Evans - Antarctic adventurer **Petty Officer Edgar ('Taffy') Evans** of the Royal Navy [died 1912] left his stone terraced house at 82 High Street, Swanage (postcode BH19 2NY) to join *Discovery* and Captain Robert Falcon Scott's expedition to the South Pole [1910].

Evans, as the plaque on the house records, was one of the five chosen to make "the final assault on the Pole, which was reached on 18 January

1912. All five men died on the 800 mile return journey across the ice ... 'To strive, to seek, to find and not to yield'."

Scott and his four gallant comrades perished in March 1912. They had been beaten to the target by Norwegian Roald Amundsen, his four companions and 17 huskies, who had arrived at the Pole on 14 December 1911. Scott had chosen not to take dogs and the five Britons each pushed a sledge weighing 190 pounds but containing inadequate rations. They starved to death in a blizzard in the attempt at returning to their ship.

Fanny - bound for London from Wales in the late eighteenth century, this vessel sank half a mile east of Peveril Point [January 1793]. She was carrying a cargo of lead, in two-hundredweight ingots, some of which were lifted and brought ashore by Eddie Bennett in 1979. Although there was unlikely to be a claimant after all this time, the Receiver of Wrecks held the salvaged lead for a year and day, which is the statutory time that has to elapse before the finder is keeper.

Forest Queen - Christmas turned into tragedy [26 December 1886] for the six crewmen of this brigantine, en route down the Channel from Antwerp with a cargo of phosphate bound for Silloth, Cumbria.

She was being driven into the south-eastern corner of Swanage's rocky cliffs, between Anvil Point and Durlston Head. The crew decided to abandon ship but the gale-force wind was from the south-east and piling a tremendous sea into the gully between Anvil Point and Tilly Whim Caves. They managed to lower their boat but drowned as it was washed inshore and then pounded to pieces.

Forres School - boarding and day preparatory school, for boys and girls between 7 and 13-years-old. Its buildings are prominent on the hilltop above the west side of Northbrook Road, north of Walrond Road and opposite Beach Gardens (postcode BH19 lPR).

The school was founded in Northwood, Middlesex, by Arthur Joseph Chadwick [1908] and soon moved to the seaside [1910]. Its name commemorates Chadwick's Elginshire origins; Forres was the family's home town. Much extended, Forres School has evolved into a range of south-facing gable-ends with the central section [1919] and west wing being backed by numerous later additions to the rear.

Geology - Swanage Bay literally sections and exposes the landforms of the parish. At the north end there is the chalk ridge of the Purbeck Hills. Next come softer deposits of the colourful Wealden sands and the clays of this bed into which the broad valley has been cut.

South-eastwards are the stones for which Purbeck is famous, with ledges of so-called marble and other shelly limestones shelving out into the sea from Peveril Point.

Then comes a second bay, Durlston Bay, which is also east-facing and is in effect a cove in these harder rocks. Their best exposures are on the other side of Durlston Head, at Tilly Whim Caves, and the coastline then turns to the west at Anvil Point, rimming the stone plateau of southern Purbeck which extends to the parish boundary in a mile or so and then beyond it for a further four miles to St Alban's Head which juts out into the English Channel.

[*See also the entries for* **Dinosaurs** *and* **Durlston's first marsupials**.]

Georgian Cottage - on the east side of Church Hill (postcode BH19 1HU), just below Sir Reginald Palgrave's memorial cross. It is part of a terrace with a "W.C. 1793" keystone set in the arch of the alleyway between it and Wyvern Cottage which is the next building down the hill.

This stone has "1940" added below its eighteenth century date, to commemorate its wartime bomb-damage repairs. As a group, and with the setting of the Mill Pond and St Mary's Church below, this curving terrace comprising The Arc, Wyvern Cottage, Georgian Cottage and then numbers 4 and 2 Church Hill form perhaps the quaintest corner of old Swanage.

Ghost stories - see entries for **Godlingston** and **Newton Cottage**

Giant's Grave and Giant's Trencher - pair of circular mounds on Godlingston Hill above the Ulwell Gap (Ordnance Survey map reference SZ 012 811). They would be presumed to be of Bronze Age date, and to have been burial mounds, but for the fact that the antiquarian J.H. Austen dug them in the nineteenth century and found nothing. Empty barrows have been excavated elsewhere in Dorset and raise the possibility of cenotaphs.

Gibbet Stone - from Court Hill, see entry for **Tithe Barn Museum**

The Globe - at the end of Durlston Head (Ordnance Survey map reference SZ 035 772) is one of George Burt's information stones: "Above sea 111 ft." Just around the corner you come to a flight of steps to the Great Globe.

This is a forty-ton sphere, ten feet in diameter, carved in Portland stone with continents, oceans and rivers. It was made in sections at the late John Mowlem's Greenwich works in 1887, and brought to Swanage in fifteen segments. It is "Above sea 136 ft."

[*See entry for* **Durlston Inscriptions.**]

Godlingston ghost story - Mrs Jean Bowerman of Godlingston Manor recorded her experience of a face at an ancient window in the Farmer's Weekly of 29 September 1967. She had been told of the ghost of a lady who was supposed to walk by the garden wall, "but seven years ago, I think, she decided to look in through a window when I was working late. I didn't see her, but had I been a dog, my hair would have stood on end as I felt her presence. Not appreciating the feeling, I fled."

Mrs Bowerman gradually forgot her experience until a former occupant of Godlingston came to tea: during conversation, this lady said that her husband had seen the ghost through the same window. "Now, alas, the ghost seems to have taken a fancy to the upstairs landing and she's even more of a deterrent than the slugs to going down at night. Not that I'm afraid - let's just say that I prefer not to look behind me on the landing."

Godlingston Manor - the oldest building in the parish of Swanage, with more ancient stonework than the parish church, this fortified country house stands to the west of Ulwell (Ordnance Survey map reference SZ 015 802).

Its south-facing frontage, with walls three feet thick, date from about 1300. This is a single-storey with stone-slated roof and three dormer windows set into the attic rooms.

What is remarkable is the contemporary rounded tower attached to the west end of the original rectangular manor house. This has solid walls of stone five feet thick on all but the side attached to the main building. The tower must have been intended as defensible, if only as a refuge in times of trouble.

The whole building may have been fortified, given that its appearance has changed with the insertion of seventeenth century stone mullioned windows and the addition of an eighteenth century north-west wing and a rebuilt cross-wing at the east end.

That it has survived at all is fortuitous, given that in 1867 it was threatened with demolition. Thomas Bond wrote: "I lament to add that these interesting remains have been permitted to fall into a sad state of dilapidation, and it is now contemplated to sweep them all away, to make room for a brand new farm-house, fit for the requirements of the agricultural magnates of the present day, who have wants unknown to the Purbeck gentry of times gone by. Such destruction will be deplored by every-one who has any regard for mediaeval architecture, or even for what is merely picturesque."

Godlingston survived and came into National Trust ownership when the charity inherited the 16,000 acres of the Kingston Lacy and Corfe Castle Estates owned by Ralph Bankes [1902-81]. It is not open to the public but the historically interesting south side is clearly visible from Swanage public footpath number 79 which goes up to its eastern end from Washpond Lane, and then the building is touchable from public footpath number 2 which passes the full length of the frontage.

Golf Club - see entry for **Enid Blyton**

Great Globe - see entry for **The Globe**

Great storm - with westerly winds recorded at 110 mph at Land's End and 105 mph on Dartmoor, the most serious of the late twentieth century hurricanes gusted across the West Country and had lost none of its ferocity on arrival in Swanage, mid-morning Thursday 25 January 1990.

As well as the usual gale-torn debris of branches, tiles, and fences, whole sections of roofs were ripped off, and the entire inflatable sports hall at the town's Harrow International Language and Sports Centre took to the sky. Its giant dome, complete with equipment, ended up in nearby tennis courts. The avenue of trees on the school's approach road was uprooted, along with many single specimens throughout the town.

There was also tragedy. Retired printer John Green [1911-90] of Holmes Road, Swanage, was swept off his feet in Station Road by a freak gust and lifted into the air. He landed on his head, fracturing his skull, and died that night in Poole General Hospital.

Grosvenor - for nearly a century the elegant four-storey lines of the **Hotel Grosvenor** graced the southern sweep of Swanage Bay. Its older, eastern wing was originally **The Grove**, a "marine residence" built for the Coventry family on the site of an old quarry below Peveril Downs [1838]. Next it was the home of retired London contractor Thomas Docwra [1866]. Then Edwin Williams built **Sunnydown** and **Peveril Tower** (renamed Rockleigh) in the grounds [1892-95].

Expansion on a grand scale, into the Hotel Grosvenor, came with the Exton family who hired Nottingham architect Walter Hickson for the centre section [1902] and then the west wing [1905]. The latter was given an extended frontage by George Hardy [1927].

King George VI and wartime Prime Minister Winston Churchill hosted dinner at the Grosvenor Hotel for a galaxy of top American, British and Canadian generals after the huge Exercise Smash practice landings for the invasion of Normandy, which were held to a realistic backdrop of bombs and live firing on the look-alike beach of Studland Bay [18 April 1944].

Closure and demolition [1985-86] were a result of a controversial and abortive attempt by Durrant Developments to replace the Grosvenor with a yacht marina and yuppy seaside village. Some luxury continental-style villas were built [1987] but receivership saw the collapse of the more grandiose plans.

The Grosvenor remains of fond memory, as Swanage author Merle Chacksfield sums up: "I certainly miss its gracious lines which added to the 'tone' of Swanage Bay. I shall always remember the evening sunlight shining on those elegant buildings bordering the deep turquoise of the sea and happy times I have spent there with my mother taking afternoon tea in its quiet, relaxed surroundings."

Groynes - wooden series of barriers set at ninety degrees to the beach, stemming tidal drift though initially resisted and resented for spoiling the sweep of the sands [1926].

Half Moon - inaccessible cove in the rocks beneath the National Trust's Belle Vue Cliffs (Ordnance Survey map reference SZ 016 768), named for its shape.

Hancock - comedian **Tony Hancock** [1924-68] went to school in Swanage, boarding at Durlston Court. He had moved to Bournemouth from Birmingham at the age of three. With the onset of puberty he became introverted. He took up acting during the war, with the RAF Gang Show.
Radio fame came as tutor in *Educating Archie* [1951-53], bringing his own show *Hancock's Half Hour* [1954-63] which transferred to television in 1956. Film roles included *The Rebel* [1961] and *The Punch and Judy Man* [1963].
He was a chain-smoking perfectionist, called "the anxiety man" by the newspapers, who found it difficult to incorporate women in his act. He killed himself in Sydney in 1968.

Hardy - author **Thomas Hardy** [1840-1928] lived in Swanage at **West End Cottage,** then the home of "an invalid captain of smacks and ketches". This provided Thomas and first wife Emma with lodgings for the autumn and winter of 1875-76.
This period widened his experience of tragedy with occasional bodies that came in naked with the sea. "The sea undresses them," ships' masters told him, about the victims of drownings that floated in with the tide from Portland and the west.
"He has read well who has learnt that there is more to read outside books than in them," Hardy wrote in his diary. That winter he finished *The Hand of Ethelberta.*

West End Cottage survives, in a cul-de-sac off Seymer Road, west of Peveril Downs open space (Ordnance Survey map reference SZ 034 785).

Hardy is also said to have been involved in the design of St Mark's Church, Herston, during his early working life as an architect.

Hardy would return to Swanage on 31 October 1919 to join the Bishop of Salisbury in opening Swanage Children's Hospital at Hill Side, Peveril Road.

Hardy - construction engineer **William Masters Hardy** built the sea-wall at Ramsgate [1871]. It was "1,700 feet long and 22 feet high, at the bottom of the chalk-cliff on the west side of Ramsgate Harbour". He was also a builder in his home town of Swanage and restored Studland Parish Church [1881].

In retirement he filled his days with writing into advanced old age, becoming the first Swanage historian and leaving a wealth of memories and contemporary anecdotes, preserved along with numerous delightful stories in a compelling series of publications.

Smuggling Days in Purbeck [1906] was followed by a full-size history of *Old Swanage and Purbeck* [1908; expanded edition 1910]. He also wrote about *Wave Action on our Coast* [1911] and produced a number of pamphlets.

Heather Close - see entry for **Newton Cottage**

Holiday resort and paddle-steamers - it was George Burt, the rough-speaking baron of the stone trade, who saw the future of Swanage as a respectable watering place. One thing was lacking - there was no railway. The main line between Southampton and Dorchester had been completed in May 1847 and passed through Wareham. The Isle of Purbeck Railway, a branch extension, was proposed in 1862 and accepted by Parliament the following year. But nothing came of it.

George Burt applied himself again to the project after John Mowlem's death in 1868. Then, when he had failed to bring the railway, he was astute enough to provide an alternative and bought a steam boat to run between Swanage and Bournemouth. She was the *Heather Bell* and operated from 1871 to 1877. Burt said in 1880:

"Bournemouth people were originally rather jealous of my steamboat, but in the course of a year or two they found people said, 'Is that steamboat running now? If she is, I shall come to Bournemouth. If she is not, I shall not come.' There is no doubt about it - Bournemouth people now say if more people could get over to Swanage they would have more visitors come to Bournemouth."

Summer 1880 was when the steamer really discovered Swanage. It was the year that saw the opening of a new pier at Bournemouth and it was from there that most of the visitors came. *Heather Bell* had been the pioneer steamer in May 1871. Then *Lothair* took on the route between Swanage and Poole, with up to four journeys weekly, but 1880 was the season she was sold and left for the shores of Greece. *Telegraph* continued to run and came on Mondays and Thursdays. *Sunshine* arrived in March that year and brought sixty passengers, most of them bound for Corfe Castle. Later in the season there were protests at Sabbath-breaking by Sunday excursions and she gave up and returned to Liverpool. In June the Bournemouth Steam Packet Company introduced a new steamer, the *Carham*, to the Swanage route. *Princess* started to call whilst en route between Weymouth and the Isle of Wight. Lastly, there was *Florence*. She, alone, anchored at Swanage pier each night and was regarded as the town's own steamer.

In August 1880 it was reported from Swanage that "several hundreds are daily carried to Bournemouth or the Isle of Wight" but with winter coming the excursions ceased and the town felt its previous isolation.

The paddle-steamer that took over the main run between Bournemouth and Swanage in 1881, and for the next three decades, was the *Lord Elgin*. Minor summer services from elsewhere included the *Telegraph* which plied from Poole, via Sandbanks, on a sixpenny ticket.

Swanage was to be a late developer among the Victorian coastal resorts, and had to promote its new-found attractions to the full. The foremost propaganda initiative was the publication of *Swanage*, an unreliable book edited by John Braye, in 1890. It praises the achievements of George Burt who is given credit for transfiguring the town "to such an extent that those who knew it fifteen years ago would scarcely recognise it, were it not for the ancient landmarks".

Unrelieved sedateness and the opinion that Swanage could offer paradise to invalids ripple through the pages of the book. The town laid a determined claim to be an idyllic health resort and bathing machines were far from being all it offered. Enthusiasm for the town's climate was the basic theme: "The range of temperature of Swanage being so small compared with most places, the air being so bracing and dry, and the nearly total absence of fog, frost, and snow should bring the little town to the notice of all seeking a healthy spot, whether to go and settle down indefinitely or during the colder months of the year."

Quietude was another virtue and Swanage differed from the fashionable watering places in lacking "the terrible noise occasioned by German bands or strolling nigger companies". Such nuisances, the writer lamented, had become the pest of not only English resorts but their continental counterparts.

Ventnor was one of the most successful of Victorian resorts and came in for the envy of Swanage. All manner of statistics were thrown against the Isle of Wight town, and a conclusion that hit at Bournemouth for good measure: "One great disadvantage is that it [Ventnor, Isle of Wight] is overrun with invalids of every description, which is very depressing. Bournemouth, though on the opposite side to Swanage, is in no way so good a residence for invalids. The air is much too relaxing, and after staying there a short time the invalid feels this. There is a want of the tonic air so conspicuous in Swanage. I would also mention the comparative warmness of the Swanage minimum temperature, throughout the year, as compared with Bournemouth, and hence of course the smallness of range at Swanage. Many of the invalids from Bournemouth will probably migrate over to Swanage as time rolls on."

Paddle-steamers survived the Second World War but were losing their mass appeal in the 1950s, as some of the clientele discovered holiday camps and aviation widened the overseas horizons. The last regular service ended in 1964, with the non-appearance of the steamers making news in 1965: "*Consul*, Britain's oldest paddle-steamer, has ploughed the seas from Weymouth to Bournemouth since 1897. But she has been losing money for the past two years and her owners, Cosens and Co., are to lay her up at Weymouth. This year, for the first time in living memory, there will be no paddle steamer trips to Lulworth Cove."

Subsequently, the Paddle Steamer Preservation Society revived the experience, with nostalgic returns of the Clyde-based *Waverley*, the last ocean-going paddle steamer and a relative youngster in that she was the post-war government-provided replacement for her namesake lost in the Dunkirk evacuation of May 1940.

Hospital - the Victorian **Cottage Hospital** in Queen's Road, "a neat building of Purbeck stone," was erected as a memorial to George and Elizabeth Burt by their surviving children. Opened on 26 September 1895, it contained 16 public beds and two private wards. It has now expanded into Swanage Hospital.

Iliffe - newly-wed **Jean Iliffe,** the former twice-widowed Mrs Jean King [1926-73] of Grosvenor Road, Swanage, still had a soft spot for her former American boy friend. Eighteen days after her wedding to engineer **Terence Iliffe** [born 1921], his fourth marriage, she played *Spanish Eyes* on the record deck. It was their song; the one that brought back memories of Joe Grygiel. She proceeded to phone him in America. "I love you," she said. "I have always loved you."

Mr Iliffe said that his wife then threw a book at him: "She taunted me; she said I was not quite up to standard in sexual matters. She kept talking about Joe."

Events in the Grosvenor Road household, which had been Mrs Iliffe's home for a number of years, deteriorated into a fracas and worse [3 December 1973]. Mr Iliffe punched and strangled her, it would be alleged.

Mrs Iliffe failed to make her customary phone call to her mother, who alerted the police. A constable found Mr Iliffe in the kitchen. He was covered in blood from haemorrhaging induced by a drugs overdose. He kept muttering "Jean". Then he lost consciousness and was taken to a London hospital. Around the house police found no less than eight suicide notes in Mr Iliffe's clear handwriting.

They also found Jean. She was in the kitchen freezer. The hospital managed to save Terence's life and he stood trial for murder at Winchester Crown Court [1974]. Balding, with long grey sideburns, immaculate in his suit, he looked and spoke like a successful bank manager. He denied murder but would be convicted on a majority verdict of 10-2.

He was sentenced to life imprisonment, with Mr Justice Wien remarking that he would have passed the same sentence even if the jury had cleared him of murder and found him guilty of manslaughter instead.

Terence's daughter, from his second marriage which ended with that wife's suicide [1967], was at Sherborne School for Girls, and Colin Graham of Dorset County Magazine was asked by Mr Iliffe to send him a photograph of the school. "I am indeed most grateful for the excellent photograph," he wrote from Winchester prison. "In fact I made a sketch of it and sent it to Angela."

He also sent me a letter in support of the campaign - then at its peak - for the release of the Purbeck coastal army ranges:

"I was reading an old Telegraph magazine and read about your campaign to win Tyneham back for the people. Being a resident of Swanage I have been down to Worbarrow on the rare occasions it has been open to us. In fact I've a cine film of Angela climbing the hill on the left of the bay and also paddling. I with others still feel angry how the Ministry of Defence have kept land they borrowed. I can only hope that you will keep up your campaign, and that you will in time be victorious and that Tyneham and the surrounding area will be handed over to the National Trust."

Isle of Purbeck Golf Club - see entry for **Enid Blyton**

Jardine - for brilliant law writer **David Jardine** [1794-1860] see entry for the **Judge's Seats**.

Jean-Marie - French brig wrecked on Peveril Point [April 1839]. Lieutenant [later Vice-Admiral] George Davies of the Royal Navy, the officer commanding Swanage Coast Guard, led a daring rescue which also involved the Revenue cutter *Tartar*.

All eight crewmen were saved and several silver medals were awarded to the rescuers.

John - Welsh impressionist painter **Augustus John** [1878-1961] had many Dorset connections. They began in Swanage in 1899 when he stayed at

Mrs Katherine Everett's boarding house, Peveril Tower, and he went back the following year to seduce Viennese aristocrat Maria Katerina: "The country here is lovely beyond words. Corfe Castle and neighbourhood would make you mad with painter's cupidity."

John returned to Peveril Tower for his honeymoon with Ida Nettleship in 1900. She would die of peritonitis in 1907 and he moved to Alderney Manor, Poole, and a debauched lifestyle that would make him a living legend.

The Judge's Seats - that on Peveril Downs is inscribed "D.J. 1852" and a similar seat with the same initials and dates at one end and "REST AND BE THANKFULL" (sic) along the side is on the top of Ballard Down, on the Studland side of the parish boundary (Ordnance Survey map reference SZ 033 813). They were erected by **David Jardine** [1794-1860], the Recorder for Bath, who came from Weybridge and had adopted the Purbeck quarry town. He paid £120 towards providing St Mary's Church with its clock [1859], which was half the cost.

He was a brilliant writer on legal history, "very learned and ingenious" to quote Macaulay who used Jardine's work as the source for his own popularisations of English history. *A Reading on the use of Torture in the Criminal Law of England previously to the Commonwealth* [1837] was followed by a study of the Gunpowder Plot and *Remarks on the Law and Expediency of requiring the presence of Accused Persons at Coroners' Inquisitions* [1846].

Jardine also provided Swanage with a policeman, John Cripps, who would come close to losing his life at the hands of the natives in a Christmas Eve riot.

Kemp - the decomposing body of Christchurch secretary **Diana Kemp** [1949-69] was discovered in a ditch at the Ulwell Gap, close to the road through the hills from Swanage to Studland and a few feet from a bus-stop below the west end of Ballard Down [30 November 1969]. She was wearing the remains of a blue mini-dress but her underwear and stockings were missing.

Diana had left her home in Elizabeth Avenue, Christchurch, at 8.15 pm on Thursday 16 October 1969. Her parents assumed she had gone out to see her boy friend, Robert, whom she telephoned earlier in the evening, but that was to make an arrangement to meet him outside Christchurch Town Hall at 7.30 pm the following evening.

She never returned home on the Thursday. At about 8.35 that night two young men found her shoulder bag, lying on the main road at Rushford Warren, Mudeford. They found her address in it and took it to her home.

Diana, who worked for Goadsby and Harding estate agents in Bournemouth, was described by her mother as "the centre of attention" at parties. The hope was that as she suffered glandular fever she might have lost her memory. They realised, however, that there was more to it than that. As her father said: "After all, a handbag is a girl's most treasured possession."

She was known to have a dangerous predilection for hitch-hiking but between Diana's disappearance and the discovery of her body no one came to the police's attention as a suspect. Nor had there been any sightings.

"But where's Diana's watch?" her mother asked when she was told about the discovery of the body.

The watch was in Ashley Road Furniture Centre at 170-172 Ashley Road, Parkstone.

Not only did dealer David Taylor have Diana's Pontiac brand lady's wrist watch, which he had bought from a 25-year-old, giving him a £1 note [26 November 1969] but he also recalled the young man's conversation. He had noticed a tape recorder in the window, saying it was like a friend's machine. This was a long-shot but the police decided to follow up the tape recorder lead - their first in a search that had dragged on for weeks and was now a murder hunt.

Everything started to fall into place. Not only had Mr Taylor written down the 19-year-old seller's name and address. It then turned out that this young man had a 25-year-old friend and they had been working together as cinema projectionists at the Regent in Christchurch.

Police traced the friend to lodgings in Westbourne but found he had just departed in a white Hillman. He had, however, left a forwarding address.

Two days later [8 December 1969], Ian George Troup would be arrested in Dulwich. In his car were copies of newspapers carrying news of the discovery of Diana's body.

Mr Troup admitted selling the watch but said that he had found it in Boscombe Gardens. He turned out to be something of a loner, who liked Swanage - indeed he said he had lived there - and had been spending much of his time model-making, invariably ships from plastic kits.

He stood trial at Winchester where he pleaded not guilty to murder but admitted struggling with Diana Kemp, after she had declined to have sex with him at Mudeford, and then driving to Swanage to dump the body when he found she had died.

The jury convicted him of murder and he was sentenced to life imprisonment [12 March 1970].

Knollsea - the fictional name for Swanage in the writings of Thomas Hardy [*see his entry*].

Kyarra - 4,383-ton merchant ship of the Australian United Steamship Company, torpedoed by a German U-boat at the start of her return journey from Southampton to Sydney on 5 May 1918. She sank into an upright position in a hundred feet of water a mile and a half off Durlston Head. Nine died. Earlier in the Great War she had operated off Belgium as a floating hospital.

The wreck, which stands to thirty feet, was discovered by a woman from London in the late 1960s and then bought by her diving club, though only limited salvage work has been carried out by the club. The ship was comparatively modern, having been built on the Clyde in 1903.

She has since claimed a further life. Marine artist and photographer Martin Pilcher, aged 44 of Lilliput, Poole, drowned whilst diving on the *Kyarra* [1992].

Further out from her at Durlston are the wrecks of the *Forth Fisher*, the *Avanti*, *Carrantan*, and the collier *Castlereagh* which went down in 1925.

Lifeboat - the decision to accede to petitions from Swanage for a lifeboat was agreed by the London committee of the Royal National Life-Boat

Institution [4 March 1875]. Conveniently there were unplaced funds, in the form of a bequest from Miss Margaret Ryder Wilde, via her nephew Samuel J. Wilde of Serjeant's Inn, with the request from his aunt that a new lifeboat should be named *Charlotte Mary* in memory of her two sisters.

The local committee that did the organising in 1875 had Mr (later Sir) J.C. Robinson as its patron, George Burt as president, Mr (later Sir) Reginald Palgrave as vice-president, and members Henry Burt, H.J. Hixson (Burt's steward), Richard Haynes (of Magnolia House), John Haysom (Purbeck Hotel), George Horlock (Postmaster), William Trayte (Robinson's steward) and James Pope (Banker).

The Earl of Eldon gave a plot of foreshore at the south-east corner of Swanage Bay (Ordnance Survey map reference SZ 039 786) protected from the prevailing winds by Peveril Downs and from the south-easterlies by Peveril Point which projected seawards 250 yards to the east. The lifeboat-house cost £350 and its slipway £175. It and the boat were very quickly in service, being declared open and *Charlotte Mary* duly named on 16 September 1875, by Mrs Samuel Wilde.

The second Swanage lifeboat, larger at 37-feet and with twelve oars, was the *William Erle*, named by her donor, Lady Erle, in memory of Chief Justice Sir William Erle [December 1890]. The crew rejected the vessel, claiming it was unstable, and a replacement, also called *William Erle*, arrived in 1893.

Her first rescue attempt, into a blizzard, had to be called off when the coxswain, William Brown, was swept to his death off Old Harry Rocks, into a turbulent and confused sea that nearly claimed the lifeboat as well [12 January 1895].

Despite this sad start, she handled well, and rescued many, until retirement through old age in 1914.

The self-righting *Zaida* was next, secondhand from Carrickfergus, and replaced by *Herbert Sturmey* [presented 10 October 1918], named for the deceased benefactor. Also self-righting, she was one of the last sailing lifeboats to be constructed.

Thomas Markby was not only a bit longer, at 40-feet, but had an engine. Just about the whole town were on Peveril Point to watch her launched down a reconstructed slipway [7 July 1928]. She would survive numerous call-outs, including 12 hours in 70 mph winds out of which, in Lyme Bay, she towed the yacht *Pauamma* to safety in Weymouth [4 July 1937]. *Thomas Markby* also survived the Second World War and its interminable searches in seas that were patrolled by the Luftwaffe.

On retirement [1949] she was replaced by a Watson-class 41-feet vessel with 35hp engines which was named R.L.P. for a member of the Pugh family from Kensington.

For local lifeboat centenary year [1975] Swanage received its eighth boat, the 38-feet Rother class *J. Reginald Corah*, named for a Leicester industrialist who died in 1955. Lew Hardy was the onshore co-ordinator for rescues, and someone asked him the wrong question at the centenary celebrations.

"There's nothing glamorous about putting out to sea in bad weather to search half the night for a missing boat," he told the reporter.

The boat-house was extended and provided with a new slipway [1991] for a Mersey class lifeboat, *Robert Charles Brown* - named for a long-standing coxswain - which cost £350,000, raised by the local Royal National Lifeboat Institution appeals group. Capable of 16.5 knots, with a reinforced resin hull, she carries a minimum crew of five and has a seven minute turn-out time. As well as satellite navigation, radar and depth-sounding equipment she carries a VHF direction finder to home-in on the radio signal of a vessel in distress.

Major incidents are described in this book under the names of the stricken vessels concerned. By the late twentieth century, however, call-outs were generally for yachtsmen and other weekend sailors. Not that dangers are any less for the lifeboat crew, nor the seamanship required of them, as a rescue in October 1976 showed.

The Swanage lifeboat was launched into conditions described as "the worst for over thirty years" to save the lives of two men in a French yacht, which resulted in Purbeck boatmen Ron Hardy and Victor Marsh being awarded the Lifeboat Institution's bronze medal for gallantry. Their lifeboat was damaged in the rescue, and but for the skill of the men's manoeuvring, could have been lost.

As the boat was being pounded violently by the waves, Mr Marsh risked his life in attempting to remove a rope that had fouled the propeller. Crew members Tom Haw, George Bishop, Eric Dorey, Pete Hardy and

Ian Marsh also received certificates in recognition of their part in the rescue.

The lifesaving of 14 October started when the Russian trawler *Topaz* spotted the French yacht in difficulties and took her in tow. The trawler then radioed British coastguards to take over the rescue. Swanage lifeboat met the trawler off Peveril Point but language difficulties prevented the operation going smoothly.

By that time, a force-ten gale raged, with a rise and fall of up to twenty feet between waves and troughs. Lines had to be secured, and a rope ladder lowered from the side of the trawler. The first Frenchman climbed down and jumped aboard the lifeboat but it took several journeys up and down the ladder before the second man had enough confidence to leap aboard.

The lifeboat then picked up the yacht's tow-rope, but the lifeboat's rudder and propeller became fouled. The yacht had to be cut clear. Victor Marsh then tried to clear the propeller with a freeing tool but this task was extremely difficult because the boat was rolling violently, and the waves were smashing through the scuttle and over the stern.

Hardy, the coxswain, decided to make for Swanage on only one engine, and put a member of his crew on to the yacht with a drogue made of old ropes. Because of the conditions, the two boats had to head further north to the calmer waters of Poole Harbour, and the drogue successfully controlled the yacht, except as she was crossing the shallow sands of the Bar off Shell Bay.

At Poole a diver cleared the lifeboat's fouled propeller. There was damage to the lifeboat but this could have been "much more serious but for Coxswain Hardy's superb seamanship. Without Victor Marsh's attempt to clear the propeller and his prudent checking of the other propeller shaft, the lifeboat could easily have been left in the storm without power."

Lighthouse - built on Anvil Point (Ordnance Survey map reference SZ 029 769) by Trinity House in 1880-82. Lighthouse Road, constructed from the outskirts of the town at Sunnydale Road, is its mile long access road.

Lock-up - see entry for the **Town Hall**

London street furniture - not for nothing is Swanage known as "Little London by the Sea" for as well as transplanting whole landmarks, such as the Town Hall, Clock Tower, and Ballard Down Obelisk, Victorian developer George Burt also brought home numerous lesser relics.

He literally carted off lamp standards, cannon posts, columns from Billingsgate Market, two statues from the Royal Exchange, and an archway from Grosvenor Square. Any movable landmarks from the London scene were duly uprooted, dismantled, brought home and put together again at Purbeck House or placed elsewhere across the town. Ten lamp standards on The Parade and Beach Road, for instance, were of cast iron and stamped "Saint George Hanover Square" whilst others proclaimed the "City of London". All over the Durlston estate there are cannon posts standing as bollards or supporting gates (*see the entry for Bollards*).

Lord Elgin - veteran Stockton-built [1876] single funnel 203-ton paddle-steamer of the Bournemouth-Swanage run [1881-1911] she then moved to the Solent and was the mainstay of the Southampton-Cowes cargo service until being withdrawn and scrapped [1955].

Manwell - reluctant philosopher **Thomas Manwell** [1751-1822] opted out of the greatness that could have been, according to his memorial inscription written by Swanage rector Dr. Andrew Bell.

This recorded that "unassisted by education" he had used "the strength of a superior genius, and Nature for his guide" to break through "the barrier to literature".

His "degree of knowledge" was such that it "might have ranked him with the first philosophers of the age".

Then comes Bell's "but": "Being a child of solitude, he retired. Meditations were far dearer to him than the acquirement of Fame; And if Charity, Humility, and Meekness, with Faith in a Redeemer, be Christianity, he was a perfect Christian."

Manwell died on 4 February 1822, leaving behind sundials rather than words, one of them being placed on St Mary's Church. He must have made some impact on his times in that the lane where he lived has since carried his name. Manwell's Lane (postcode BH19 2RA) is on the south side of the High Street, west of the Black Swan. Adjoining it are now Manwell Road and Manwell Drive.

Marine Villas - on the Pier approach at the east end of the High Street (postcode BH19 2AP), these were originally a single Marine Villa which was built by William Morton Pitt as his seaside summer house [1825].

Stucco rendered and embellished with attractive wrought-iron trelliswork porches, this Regency building was erected purely for pleasure - with baths, billiard room and coffee room - and entertained the Duke of Gloucester and a party of well-heeled yachtsmen who arrived from Lulworth Cove during their stay at Lulworth Castle [1828].

Mellor - politician **David Mellor** [born 1949], the son of Wareham mathematics teacher Douglas H. Mellor, would become the best known old boy of the former Swanage Grammar School. Remembered as a "precious little swot", he left to study law at Cambridge, and was called to the bar [1972].

He was chosen, in preference to his close friend and contemporary John Major, to fight the Labour-held seat of Putney [1974]. Five years later he was in the House of Commons [1979] and then, though only 33, became the first of that intake to climb the ministerial ladder [1981].

"One of the most promising political careers of modern times" saw him rise to become Minister for the Arts and then Secretary of State for the Heritage [April 1992] which encompassed sport as well as culture and led to the tabloid press dubbing him the "Fun Minister".

Ivan Fallon would chart his final two months in office in the Sunday Times [27 September 1992]: "In many ways his was the classic case of hubris, an excess of ambition and pride which would inevitably lead to ruin. There is nothing lean and hungry about him - indeed, his podginess is the true reflection of a practised sybarite. He struck his critics forcibly as overly ambitious, self-satisfied and cocky, the type of man that needed to be taken down a peg or two."

The first peg would be in the shapely form of Antonia de Sancha, resulting in headlines such as "DAVID MELLOR AND THE ACTRESS

- MELLOR MADE LOVE IN CHELSEA STRIP! - TOE JOB TO NO JOB".

"MELLOR QUITS AT LAST" came after he had been hit by a second story - "the double wammy" - with revelations that Palestinian film producer Mona Bauwens had treated the Mellor family to a fortnight in Marbella. That was innocent enough, but clouded with guilt by association as their host was the daughter of the Palestinian Liberation Organisation's finance chief Jaweed al-Ghussein and the holiday coincided with the Gulf War. Potentially sensitive, it had not been cleared with then Prime Minister Margaret Thatcher, and the press had another dose of front pages: "TOP TORY AND THE PLO PAYMASTER."

In his resignation speech to Parliament, Mellor said he was leaving the "warmth of government for the icy wastes of the back benches", ending with a reference to another Putney man, Titus Oates of the Antarctic.

Famous last words would be recalled: "I am going out and it may be some time before I return."

Methodist Church - set back from the High Street, on the south side, about 200 yards south-east of St Mary's Church (Ordnance survey map reference SZ 029 787).

This splendid structure is the best Victorian gothic [1886] in town, overflowering with tracery that rises into a tower and then a steeple. It preserves the foundation stone of the earlier "WESLEYAN CHAPEL BUILT 1807 ENLARGED 1842" re-set in the east wall of the present car-park. The main church has its stones at the corners.

On the east side: "This stone was laid by G. Burt Esq. J.P. Aug 14th 1885 ... This stone was laid by G.E. Robinson Esq. Aug 14th 1885."

On the west side: "This stone was laid by Mrs Jobson of London. Relict of the Rev. F Jobson D.D. Aug 14th 1885 ... This stone was laid by Sir W.M. Arthur K.C.M.G., M.P. Aug 14th 1885."

Burt also puts in an appearance, literally, carved over the entrance, together with Wesleyan minister Rev George Terry. Their faces are life size and both bearded but set high, on each side of the main window, where they are not immediately noticeable.

A brass on marble plaque to Rev George Terry is just inside the door: "THIS TABLET IS PLACED HERE BY GEORGE BURT OF

PURBECK HOUSE IN THE JUBILEE YEAR OF QUEEN VICTORIA'S REIGN IN RECOGNITION OF THE SERVICES RENDERED IN THE INTERESTS OF METHODISM IN SWANAGE BY THE REVD. GEORGE TERRY B.A. WHO UNDER THE BLESSING OF GOD BY HIS OWN INDOMITABLE COURAGE AND ENERGY AND WITH THE CO-OPERATION OF SYMPATHETIC FRIENDS SUCCEEDED IN SECURING THE SITE ERECTING THE BUILDING AND OBTAINING THE GREATER PORTION OF THE FUNDS OF THIS SO-CALLED WESLEY MEMORIAL CHURCH AS COMMEMORATING THE VISITS OF JOHN WESLEY TO SWANAGE 100-YEARS-AGO. AUGUST 1887."

Inside, on the west wall of the church, is a matching tablet to the stone contractor himself who, in memory of his grandmother, added the superb gothic spire to the building: "GEORGE BURT ESQUIRE JUSTICE OF THE PEACE FOR DORSET AND MIDDLESEX IN WESTMINSTER EX-SHERIFF OF LONDON AND MIDDLESEX AND ONE OF HER MAJESTY'S LIEUTENANTS FOR THE CITY OF LONDON GAVE THE SPIRE OF THIS CHURCH IN AFFECTIONATE MEMORY OF HIS GRANDMOTHER MARY BURT."

The earlier Burts have their memorials on the opposite wall. Robert Burt [died 1825, aged 75] was husband of Mary Burt [died 13 March 1826, aged 85]. The latter: "HAVING WALKED TO SALISBURY AND BROUGHT THE REVD. JOHN WESLEY ON HIS FIRST VISIT TO SWANAGE SHE BECAME ONE OF HIS FOLLOWERS AND REMAINED SO UNTIL HER DEATH, A PERIOD OF FIFTY YEARS."

Matching in style, the "Wesley Centenary Hall and Sunday School" were added on the east side of the church in 1907. It has a line of dedication stones including one to "Mr Moses Manwell aged 90. Local Preacher 60 years."

Mile posts - the prominent white-painted steel pole at Anvil Point (Ordnance Survey map reference SZ 029 769) and a similar one a nautical mile to the west, on the cliffs south of Verney Farm (SZ 012 769), were erected for speed calculations in naval sea trials.

Mills - bank manager **Horace Albert Mills** of the Westminster Bank, 1 Institute Road, was "killed by enemy action" on 17 August 1942 at the age of 53. He is buried in Swanage Cemetery, Washpond Lane, Godlingston.

Monarch - a double-funnel paddle-steamer of Cosens and Company, Weymouth, which was assigned to the Bournemouth-Swanage service for more than half a century [1888-1950]. She was then broken-up.

Monk-fish - common in the sea off Swanage with an extraordinary specimen, 4 feet 6 inches in length, being caught by a yachtsman near Peveril Point in June 1892. It was 2 feet 6 inches in breadth. On being cut open it was found to be a pregnant female containing "22 young ones, each measuring 10 inches in length and five inches across".

Mowlem - builder **John Mowlem** [1788-1868], founder of the major contracting company that still carries his name, was born in a cottage at Carrants Court, on Court Hill, Swanage. It was demolished in Edwardian times. Mowlem is buried in the Northbrook Road Cemetery, beneath a pyramid of his own Guernsey granite (Ordnance Survey map reference SZ 027 790). His pyramid is marvellous. Despite now having to contend with tacky modern architecture in the shape of Gilbert Court, which overlooks its wall, it is appropriately the only oversized memorial in the whole of Swanage's Victorian collection.

And how oversized! First there is an unclimbable wall of stone to stop the boys progressing further. Next is a plinth of steps. Then comes the pyramid itself, in matching blue Guernsey granite with the maker's marks in the south-west corner: "H. BISSON. VALE. GUERNSEY."

Above, twice, it says "JOHN MOWLEM'S VAULT." The words to the occupants are "JOHN MOWLEM MARCH 8th 1868 AGED 79 YEARS" and "SUSANNAH HIS WIFE NOV 11th 1849 AGED 61 YEARS". It comes to a point 20 feet above the surrounding grass.

His birthplace, a cottage on the north side of Court Hill between the High Street and Carrants Court Farm, was demolished early in the twentieth century.

Mowlem's chance in life was given him by fashionable London mason Henry Westmacott in a workshop at King's Row, Pimlico [1807]. Mowlem became his foreman [1816] but later walked out of the business and started his own [by 1823]. Soon he was leasing a wharf at Pimlico Basin [now the forecourt of Victoria Station] and paving much of the City of London. Relaying Blackfriars Bridge with Guernsey granite setts caused him so many difficulties that he took a boat to the Channel Islands and bought a one acre hillside field "all of good blue granite" which became his own quarry. Five stone dressers were employed and the granite shipped from Guernsey to London [1840]. There would be more astute land deals in Guernsey and his own brig, the *John Mowlem*, which conveyed the stone to the capital, "the great metropolis of the world" as he called it. The islanders had virtually given him the stone with which to make a fortune - one quarry cost him £50 for the freehold, which was a farthing for each of the half-a-million tons he would extract from it.

Victoria Terrace [built 1835-36] was owned by Robert Burt. Mowlem brought No.2, a three-storey lodging house, in anticipation of returning to Dorset for semi-retirement [1845].

He built and moved into the castellated Herston House at Herston [demolished 1967] and played a leading part in the construction of Swanage's first timber-built pier [1859]. Next he bought the estate extending north-westwards from the Brook to Ulwell [1860]. Mowlem then set about erecting commemorative monuments to the supposed naval battle between King Alfred and the Danes [that 877; the column 1862], and Prince Consort "Albert the Good" whose memorial [extant 1862-1971] was rediscovered by me [1992] in pieces in St Aldhelm's Quarry near St Alban's Head and photographed as proof.

The Mowlem Institute [extant 1863-1966] "for the benefit and mutual improvement of the working classes" acted as a general meeting place and cultural centre at the heart of the seafront. It has been replaced by the Mowlem Theatre, which preserves Mowlem's bust in the entrance lobby. A tablet below it records his establishment of the Mowlem Buildings.

Mowlem took on various civic duties in Swanage, filling his time as magistrate and using a highly diluted proportion of his talents to drain, level, pave and kerb the High Street and other roads. One was De Moulham Road, commemorating his family's centuries-old links with Swanage. He was a perfectionist of the trivial, fussing day-long in Swanage over the laying of the kerb stones.

The town's benefactor, he would die in the "Old" Purbeck House, High Street, Swanage [1868], in the home of his wealthy nephew George Burt. That was before John Mowlem & Co. Ltd [now Plc] started to prosper on the grand scale, beginning with the new Billingsgate Market [1874], winning royal commissions such as the refurbishment of Westminster Abbey for Edward VII's coronation [1902], and continuing with major construction work through the twentieth century, from the Dorchester bypass to the new London Bridge, and Docklands Light Railway.

The Mule Stone - perhaps the most touching of Dorset epitaphs is that on a large boulder of Purbeck stone beside the Priest's Way near Belle Vue Farm (Ordnance Survey map reference SZ 016 783). It was erected by quarryman Werney Bonfield, who built Providence Terrace, Swanage, towards the end of Victoria's reign:

"Beneath this stone lies our mule. She was a faithful creature, drawing up the stone from this quarry for 32 years. Died aged 34 years. Also our little cat named Too Too, who followed her master from this quarry to his home and back for twenty years. R.I.P."

Murders - see entries for **Diana Kemp** and **Jean Iliffe**

Name origins - see entry for **Swanwich**

National Trust land - almost the entire northern boundary of Swanage parish is National Trust owned, including Whitecliff Farm, most of Ballard Down, the Ulwell Gap, Godlingston Manor, and Godlingston Hill. On the other side of the boundary, Trust ownership extends across most of the parish of Studland, to the sea at Poole Harbour. Indeed,

Godlingston Heath - Trust-owned and now part of Studland Heath National Nature Reserve - used to be part of the parish of Swanage.

All of this land with the exception of Whitecliff Farm, where 222 acres were bought in 1976, came to the Trust as part of the 16,000-acre Kingston Lacy and Corfe Castle Estates which it inherited on the death of Ralph Bankes in 1981.

Likewise, Verney Farm came into Trust ownership, giving it the western edge of Swanage parish from the Priest's Way south to the sea. The Trust also owns Belle View Cliffs, a field distant to the east, where it bought 51 acres in 1976 with a donation from Mr L. Forder in memory of his wife, Mrs E.A.E. Forder.

Land between these two holdings, stretching inland for a mile to Herston and Gully, was added to the estate in 1994.

Naval deaths - Swanage casualties of the Great War [1914-18] included Gunner Ernest Northover on HMS *Tipperary*, Able Boatman P.J. Pesel on the cruiser HMS *Hampshire*, and Leading Seaman Frederick C. Tomes on the battleship HMS *Barham*. Able Boatman Leonard Wicks and Coast Guard Percy Milverton also failed to return home.

Naval movements - in 1855, from Peveril Point, William Masters Hardy and his friends watched the British fleet under sail for the Crimea. On 5 April 1982 their successors watched HMS *Hermes* lead two-thirds of the fighting strength of the Royal Navy to war in the South Atlantic. After both fights there was relief that it had not been worse, and in the case of the peace proclaimed with Russia in April 1856 there was a patriotic party on Peveril Downs with musicians playing and an orange and large twopenny bun for each child.

Nelson - agriculturalist **Edward Agar Horatio Nelson, fifth Earl Nelson** [1860-1951] managed landed estates but established a family home at Richmond House, 27 Rabling Road, Swanage (postcode BH19 1ED). In his youth he was a Lieutenant in the 3rd Battalion Wiltshire Regiment [1879-82] and then served in the Nile Expedition [1884-85]. He is buried in Swanage Cemetery, Washpond Lane, Godlingston.

Nelson - Ceylon tea-planter **Henry Edward Joseph Horatio Nelson, seventh Earl Nelson** [1894-1972] retired to Richmond House, 27 Rabling Road, Swanage (postcode BH19 1ED). He had served in the Australian Imperial Force in the Great War and with the Merchant Navy and as a Major in the Indian Army during the Second World War. His pastimes in his younger days were boxing and yachting. He was unmarried.

Neptune - Swanage stone boat whose sides split open - the nautical term being "bulged" - causing her to be beached and abandoned in Poole Harbour [February 1791].

Newton Cottage, renamed Heather Close - a rather plain Georgian house [built 1800] on the north side of the High Street, east of Newton Manor. Damaged by a German bomb [23 August 1942] and renovated after later demolition threats that removed its immediate neighbours [1970].

In 1804-05 it was the home of Lady Bullen, as she would become, the wife at the time of Captain Charles Bullen [1769-1853] who commanded the 100-gun HMS *Britannia*, fourth ship in the weather line that was led by HMS *Victory* in Lord Nelson's Division at the Battle of Trafalgar [21 October 1805].

Later in his career he would be knighted [1835] and advanced to the rank of Admiral [1852].

Newton Cottage ghost story - a fire in this building [*see its entry above*] was blamed on a ghost on 11 December 1966. There was "something of a ghostly nature" about the blaze, newspapers claimed, though they went on to provide a more prosaic explanation from Chief Fire Officer R.E.J. Paull: "It could have been caused by someone sleeping rough and leaving a cigarette end behind, or perhaps, by children playing with matches."

The house had been left in a time-warp, fully furnished with the beds made up, since the death of photographer William Cox was followed by that of his widow. They had left no family.

Stories of ghosts and down-and-outs were used by Swanage parents to discourage their more impressionable offspring away from a place regarded as potentially dangerous. The fire, whatever agency may have caused it, was confined to a single room and stairway.

Newton Manor - ancient seat of the Cockram family [from 1597] with seventeenth century walls hidden behind a castellated three-storey Georgian facade, added by Thomas Cockram. It stands on the north side of High Street, midway between Herston and the old part of Swanage (Ordnance Survey map reference SZ 021 789).

Interior fittings include a wealth of carvings, a staircase with scrolled balusters, and frieze-work dated 1656 and 1658 - all of which were brought to the house during its occupancy by Sir Charles Robinson, the art adviser to the Victoria and Albert Museum. After his death [1913] the house became a girls' school.

One more art object came its way, on to the roof, and is a fish weather-vane from Billingsgate Market [1850]. During its rebuilding, Victorian contractor George Burt purloined the fish as a souvenir for his new Purbeck House [1875]. It was removed to Newton Manor as a precautionary measure, having almost being blown off Purbeck House when the latter was empty after the Burt family had left [1920].

Following closure of Newton Manor School [1980] the grounds beside it, east towards Cecil Road, were redeveloped for housing.

Paddle-steamers - see entry for **Holiday resort**

Palgrave - adventure writer **Mary Palgrave** was one of the five daughters of Sir Reginald Palgrave of Hillside, Peveril Road, Swanage. In *Brave Dame Mary*, published in 1873, she produced a classic and typical Victorian tale with plenty of moral force, describing the heroism of Lady Mary Bankes who defiantly held Corfe Castle against its first Civil War siege in 1643. There is no shortage of condemnation of the Parliamentarians and with this kind of book selling tens of thousands of copies and running to many editions, it is not surprising that we were all conditioned from birth in the righteousness of the king's cause.

In *Under the Blue Flag*, Mary Palgrave moved the action to Godlingston Manor, near Ulwell Gap in the Purbeck Hills, and extended the conflict to the Duke of Monmouth's rebellion of 1685.

Palgrave - the cross at the top of Church Hill, on the north side of the High Street, Swanage, was erected in memory of **Sir Reginald Palgrave** [1829-1904], the brother of Francis Turner Palgrave [1824-97] of Lyme Regis.

Sir Reginald was Clerk of the House of Commons [1886-90]. He had written a book about Parliament, *The House of Commons: Illustrations of its History and Practice* [1869] but was better known for *The Chairman's Handbook* [1877] which ran to many editions.

He felt the Victorian age had become hysterical, his own daughter Mary Palgrave being a prime example, in its and her pathological hatred for Oliver Cromwell. This he attempted to redress with *Oliver Cromwell, the Protector: An Appreciation based on Contemporary Evidence* [1890]. Sir Reginald lived at Hillside in Peveril Road.

Parish church - see entry for **St Mary's Church**

Pentonville pillar - see entry for **Tilly Whim quotations**

Peveril Point Fort - Swanage's historic defensive position was on the promontory between its two bays, on Peveril Point, which was occupied by the Dorset Artillery Corps, part of the local volunteer forces that were the backbone of Britain's Victorian home defence. The Yeovil Gazette's Swanage correspondent reported in April 1869:

"An Artillery Corps has been formed here. Fifty-five members were sworn-in on Monday, and afterwards marched to Herston and back. Mr. J. Pope is Hon. Secretary to the corps. Lord Eldon and Mr. G. Burt have granted leases of the ground necessary for a battery and for carbine practice."

By the 1880s the corps was forty strong and "some very good firing with the big guns was made at the floating signal in the bay".

In 1968 I published an old photograph of the gun battery on Peveril Point and this led to a Purbeck diver, Bob Campbell of West Drive at Swanage, writing to let me know of his discovery of 6-inch diameter cannon balls weighing 26 lb. as well as a few 4-inch balls of 5 lb. on the floor of Swanage Bay. Before the artillery guns were stationed on the Point, there had been an earlier battery fashioned in the shape of a ship's gun deck and with a flagstaff. Two or three of its guns came from the wreck of the *Halsewell* and this battery seems to have been abandoned after a landslip in the middle of the last century. Campbell wrote in Waterspout, the Bournemouth subaqua journal:

"A recent revelation was a photograph published in the first issue of Dorset County Magazine. This showed two cannons at Peveril Point which were used by the Dorset Artillery volunteers. The presence of the clock tower and the old pier in the background dates the photograph between 1867 and 1897. The guns were mounted on large wheeled carriages and kept at the drill hall in Swanage, being dragged out to the Point with much local excitement for practice shots. They remained in use until the turn of the century. The calibre of the guns is not quoted but I recently came across some drawings of cannon which showed a thirty-two pounder gun to have a bore of 6.4 inches. This ties in with the size of ball found ... I had the good fortune to talk to an old hand who had fired these guns in his youth and he confirmed that the target, a barrel, was moored on Tanville Ledge."

The Tanville Ledge, which stretches out from the north-western section of Swanage beach off the Ocean Bay cafe, is described by John Hinchcliffe as a scenic dive:

"On a bright day the colours of the rocks, weed and fish are outstanding. In the centre of the bay is rare booty for the souvenir hunter. Careful searching will reveal a round object, the size of a large football, firmly adhering to the underlying rock and camouflaged by weed and small crustacea."

The cannon balls came from the battery on Peveril Point, established in 1558, which was enlarged in 1774 into a semi-circular arc of six guns. Target practice was at a barrel moored on the reef.

Swanage became a focal point of activity in times of national stress, such as in 1803. During the invasion scares of the Napoleonic wars, before the Battle of Trafalgar set the country at ease, about 120 volunteers met on Sundays at Swanage in Ship Lane and marched to the fort on Peveril Point, being mustered in what became Marshall Road. They were organised by Nathan Chinchen. These "Sea Fencibles" - a name derived from the Fencible Light Dragoons, disbanded in 1800 - were Pikemen.

Peveril Point battery, which contained six guns in wartime, had been built in 1774, with stone and turf barbettes beside a stone-built watch-house.

The Piers - Swanage pier, its first in the modern sense of the word though the old stone quay was also known as a pier, was built by James Walton of London [1859-60]. Swanage, then with a population of about 2,000, was still an industrial town, and a seaside tramway linked the new pier with the stone quay and quarrylands.

Swanage then had plenty of rough edges and the pier was one of them, bringing heavy criticism upon the town, such as this visitor's complaint printed in the Poole Pilot newspaper of 1 March 1869:

"Swanage is a charming place; its praises are in many mouths, and it cannot help rising in public favour if fair chances be afforded it. Its inaccessibility is one clog which retards its progress. The appearance of its Pier is by no means an attraction; its baldness and inconvenience discredit every inhabitant in the place. A more ugly, bone-breaking trap I have never looked at, especially for weak or invalid people. No side walk where passengers may go without fear of tripping between the open transverse planking, an iron tramroad projecting upwards four inches; no seat on which tired or weak people may rest whilst waiting to embark; no protection, not even a handrail, to prevent a child from falling overboard and being drowned.

"First impressions are, we all know, the most enduring, and I believe many a person has condemned Swanage immediately upon viewing this construction.

"Let me implore the Swanage inhabitants to bring their Pier Company to book during the present spring ..."

The second pier was built purely for paddle-steamers and visitors. It was constructed by Alfred Thorne of Westminster [1895-96] at a cost of £10,000 to a total length of 1,400 feet and an average width of 28 feet; "there are separate berths for vessels plying between Poole and Bournemouth and adjoining health resorts, and landing and embarking can be accomplished at any state of the tide".

As for the first pier, though increasingly rickety it continued in use until the 1920s, for coaling steamers. By the 1970s its planking had gone and the supports were rotting and disappearing into the sea.

There were fears that the second pier could go the same way until it was transferred from the receivers of Durrant Developments (Swanage Yacht Haven) Limited to Purbeck District Council for a token £1 sum [1992]. This secured their 84 per cent majority shareholding in Swanage Pier Limited and was accompanied by a reverse payment of £125,000 from the receivers to the local authority "to release them from any obligations to maintain the pier".

The Mayor of Swanage, Keith Marlow, said that with public ownership would come restoration: "I am delighted that, after the years of uncertainty which have seen the decline of the pier, a positive way forward has now emerged. This is a great step forward for Swanage and the district as a whole."

Pitcher - Chief Petty Officer **Ernest Pitcher** VC [1888-1946], who was brought up in Swanage and attended its Board School, came to fame in 1917. He was severely wounded but stayed at his gun when the armed merchantship Q50, HMS *Dunraven*, engaged a German submarine on 8 August. Pitcher was awarded the Victoria Cross; the manner of the award being unusual in that he was selected for the supreme honour by his comrades after the action in which all had shown great courage. The *Dunraven* attack was described by Lieutenant-Commander Harold Auten VC as "the greatest action of any Q-boat against a submarine. It was fought by a ship's company of heroes".

Pitcher retired from the Royal Navy in 1927 but rejoined, in 1939, to serve throughout the Second World War.

There is a memorial to him in St Mary's Church:

"In glorious memory of Chief Petty Officer Ernest Pitcher VC who was also awarded the Distinguished Service Medal the Military Medal and the Croix de Guerre for conspicuous gallantry. 1886-1946" [*sic, date of birth elsewhere given as 1888*].

His actual grave and stone are in the middle of the Northbrook Road Cemetery, inscribed to "E.J. PITCHER VC, DSM. CHIEF PETTY OFFICER RN. P/227029 H.M.S *ATTACK*. 10TH FEBRUARY 1946. AGED 57. AT THE GOING DOWN OF THE SUN AND IN THE MORNING WE SHALL REMEMBER THEM."

Pitt - philanthropist **William Morton Pitt** [1754-1836], the son of Marcia and John Pitt of Encombe, Corfe Castle, was the second of the William Pitts of the late eighteenth century. The first was an entirely different personality, the mastermind of the "Pitt and Plunder" system of British government, which created poverty and distress for Dorset cousin William to mitigate. Our Pitt inherited a vast fortune from his father and dissipated it on good works. Sir Tresham Lever, in *The House of Pitt*, writes that because of his spendings "the wealthiest branch of the family sank into the obscurity of the landless middle class".

His personal programme of social works included a cordage manufactory at Kingston, Corfe Castle, a fish-curing plant in Swanage, a spinning and bleaching school at Fordington, Dorchester, a hat-making works in the new County Gaol. He had been instrumental in its rebuilding [1787] and was delighted that in the improved regime many prisoners "are now behaving well and maintaining themselves and their families by their own industry".

He was hardly a Parliamentarian, seldom speaking in the House of Commons, but he represented Poole [1780-90] and then sat as one of the county members for Dorset [1790-1826], describing it as a career which "though not brilliant has been laborious for 45 years". He was the first chairman of the management committee of Forston House lunatic asylum, Charminster.

Somehow, through good works and bad business, he lost his great houses at Kingston Maurward, Stinsford, and Encombe, as well as Kingston village, and threw his final money and energy in converting the Manor House, Swanage, into what would be the Royal Victoria Hotel. He wrote at seventy-one that "both Mrs Pitt and I had beggarded ourselves for some time past towards the accomplishment of this object".

Police Station - like much else in Victorian Swanage, the building in Argyle Road owed its creation to shrewd developer George Burt.

Plans for the first police station at Swanage were discussed at Dorset Midsummer Sessions in Shire Hall, Dorchester, during June 1881. Burt had offered to build the station with cells and living quarters for two policemen. The cost would be £600 and Burt proposed leasing the completed building to the county for fifteen years at an annual rent of

£24. The Chief Constable, Captain Amyatt E. Amyatt, said he understood Burt also intended erecting a Town Hall close to the proposed police station and this would be available for magisterial purposes. Lord Eldon replied that the scheme to incur expense for a police station at Swanage had come as a surprise to the magistrates of the division. His reported comments were: "The present arrangement by which prisoners had to be removed from Swanage to Wareham for trial was doubtlessly inconvenient but he understood Mr Burt was going to construct a railway, and then it would be less inconvenient. (Laughter.) He was not sure the erection of this police station would be a gain. At present no petty sessions were held there, and anybody wanting to get a summons had to go to Wareham. He should like this question postponed until the next sessions in order more definite plans might be proposed."

Replying T.B. Hanham said he had known Swanage for the previous fifteen years "during which time it has completely changed". The suggested site was central and "there will be a difficulty in delaying the matter. Swanage is a place considerably increasing in value and, to my mind, it is very doubtful if the county will receive this offer again at the same price."

The meeting agreed, by one vote, not to postpone consideration of this offer, which would be duly accepted.

Prisoner of War Camp - established for German prisoners in the Great War [1916], opposite Ulwell Farm (Ordnance Survey map reference SZ 023 807), its collection of timber huts remianing in use for more than a year after the Armistice [11 November 1918].

Promenade - Edwardian topping to their recently constructed sea-wall, the foundation stone of which was laid by Sir John Mowlem Burt [25 February 1904] and survives close to the Mowlem Theatre though its inscription is no longer legible. The building was done by Sir John's family firm. Completion took place the following summer [June 1905].

Punfield Pond at Whitecliff Farm - a feature that has disappeared from Swanage shore-line, at the foot of Ballard Cliff on the north side of Swanage Bay where the chalk meets the mixed Wealden sand and clays

(Ordnance Survey map reference SZ 039 810). Here there was a large pond. It was part of Whitecliff Farm, now a National Trust property, and the farmer kept swans on it.

William Masters Hardy recounted a tradition that it had frequently been visited by King John. Boulders that contained the pond were broken up by quarrymen about 1705 to make up shortages in shipments required for repairing dikes in the Netherlands.

Punfield retains considerable interest for geologists. It is highly fossiliferous and contains the Punfield marine band which has Spanish affinities. This lies in the cretaceous layers, of the final Mesozoic period, when the lower greensand and colourful Wealden sands were accumulating in what were then tropical waters.

Purbeck Festival of Music - founded by Kato Havas [1964], with events attracting international musicians held in a variety of attractive settings, ranging from Smedmore House, Kimmeridge, and parish churches, including St Mary's Church at Swanage, to the Art Gallery at Lulworth Castle.

Purbeck House - formerly a large Georgian building at 91 High Street (postcode BH19 2NA), bought and rebuilt in Victorian gothic by George Burt [1875]. It is a rusticated extravaganza of secondhand taste with an archway from Grosvenor Place; two fifteenth century windows; iron columns; statues from the seventeenth century. Of the latter, one is from Billingsgate Market and the other two, minus legs, arms and heads, were from the ruins of the Royal Exchange which was burnt out in 1836. They feature, perhaps, Henry V and Edward I. Fragments of moulded stone and floor tiles came from the lobbies of Parliament during the rebuilding of the Palace of Westminster and include a mosaic of the Prince of Wales's motto and feather emblem with a red background and hexagonal surround.

Purbeck House was vacated by the Burt family [1920] and remained empty for many years, offers of it being declined by Swanage Urban District Council, before becoming the Convent of Our Lady of Mercy [1935].

Quarries of Swanage Townsend - the greatest stone quarry in the whole of the Isle of Purbeck was where you would today least expect to find one. Overlooking the heart of Purbeck's holiday town, strung out above the High Street in a line for nearly a mile from Bon Accord Road westward to Belle Vue Farm at Herston are the vast disused workings of Swanage Townsend: the most intensively quarried part of all Purbeck, it operated continuously from before 1700 to 1939 when Dowland's Quarry overlooking Cowlease, was the last working. The creamish-yellow stone from this broad hillside has long ago weathered to the familiar grey of Purbeck buildings, sometimes with a tinge of pink. It is one of the best known British building stones.

Although a quarry is normally an open pit, here was something quite different. Cowlease was only a small section of the workings but it was a full-scale stone mine with arms reaching 120 feet into the rock. These were the *lanes* and many were sunk in those two centuries of use. Each lane started with a *slide* - a steeply inclined shaft - and was a production line with carts taking fine limestone from passages that branched at various levels to the working faces on the *roach, thornback, cinder* (a bed of fossil oysters), *downs vein* and new vein. Each deposit of clay or loose material parting the stone beds was known as a *shiver* or just plain *dirt*.

The remains of at least twenty abandoned shafts can be seen in other parts of the three hundred acres of the Townsend quarries. This method of working started about 1700 and was adapted in the year 1800. One of the first chain cables was then made by William Coombs, a blacksmith at Court Hill, Swanage, and used by quarrymen who found it far stronger than a rope. The mine shafts were called slides because they were originally at a low angle to the ground and the first carts had no wheels and were simple sledges. With the introduction of cables the mine shafts became steeper. Though it caused draughts, the passages from two quarry lanes would occasionally connect together, making it possible to go down one shaft and surface at another hole. Underground, the ceiling was often only three feet high, though six feet was the ideal working height, and conditions were always clayey and damp. Good, hard stone had to be built up in pillars to hold the quarry roof - had a section of strata simply been left, it would have crumbled under the weight and given way. With seams being worked at several levels, the *legs* had to be solid and strong to prevent *founders*.

There were times when pieces of Swanage fell through a quarry roof. As John T. Dean reminded me, the only truly safe untouched island of land to the south of the High Street is the Cottage Hospital, the ground for which George Burt gave the town. Elsewhere, he said, the land is literally undermined:

"It is still possible to lose a walking stick whilst walking up there - it just falls down almost anywhere, out of sight. My great-uncle Tom grazed his baker's horse there for years. One Sunday just after the Great War, he was actually watching it, when it just dropped out of sight where it stood. It went down twenty-nine feet, its hind-quarters stuck, and despite ten men digging had to be shot five hours later. Certainly entire houses will drop up there, such as the twin house to Sentryfields, at the top of Seymer Road, which although identical in size, disappeared entirely just before the Great War. It is not the weight of the houses; it is all on the move anyway."

In about 1895 the western house of Alexandra Terrace collapsed into an eastern lane from the Cowlease. But, generally, the workmanship of the old men is still standing surprisingly well and the quarry legs, even as they powder, hold parts of residential Swanage proudly in the sunlight. The spreading Townsend housing estate has covered the lower edge of the quarrylands and elsewhere it is blackthorn and brambles that obscure the openings to the slides. Ivy smothers old work huts and everywhere are the heaps of overburden and *spawls*. These mounds of stone waste were also known as *scar-heaps*.

Mounds and craters cover the entire hillside rising above the southern side of Swanage. The larger hillocks mark the continuous surface workings and even at the top of the ridge you can look across to further pits beyond California Farm. Even to the west of the Townsend quarries - either side of the Priest's Way and the seemingly normal fields beyond the Swanage parish boundary at Verney Farm and to South Barn, and then along the track beside Leeson Park - most of this slope is undermined and the openings of fifteen shafts are still visible.

Above the High Street from Chapel Lane to Bell Street, the town's tentacles of bungalow development have moved up the hill, but a wasteland lies above. Because of the danger from old workings caving in, planning permission has been consistently refused for any building further up the hillside. This has been to the town's advantage as a natural, if pockmarked, skyline can be seen to the south of Swanage and it is better to look up at a green hill than watch buildings clamber over to the next obstacle. The view in reverse, from any part of the slopes, overlooks the entire Swanage valley with the town distended from right to left, strung out along the High Street from the shore to Herston. Here Pat Henshaw discovered a narrow gauge mineral railway in the form of "a short rope-worked incline" used to take stone "from a group of quarries to a sawmill".

It is hard to visualise this as the heart of a great industry. All the workings are abandoned and the grass-grown spoil heaps that heave everywhere seem tossed imperceptibly together, and each dip is filled with dense clumps of thorn, bramble and elder. All the shafts have been partially or completely filled and the biggest hole remaining in the early 1970s was a few yards from the bungalows, a short distance southeast of the end of Hillside Road and just east of the old stone wall that is now the boundary of Swanage urban council's caravan site. The nearby Grandfather's Knap is the biggest of the *spawl* heaps, accumulated from six quarries over forty years.

In *Purbeck Island* in 1972 I described this area of industrial archaeology and called for its preservation:

"This shaft is thirty feet wide and twenty feet deep with three sheer sides of the natural rock reinforced with drystone walling: a pit in which the body of a discarded car looks quite small. From the fourth side, the north, a wide and steep shaft rises from the bottom. A few feet northward from its head stands a perfectly preserved capstan with its stones complete but the wooden parts, as would be expected, have rotted away. Around these historic stones, and hiding them from attention, is a thick clump of bushes. It was only after two days of searching, and when winter had lessened the screen, that I found this relic. A century ago, chains from its horse-operated hub were raising stone by the ton, but it is now the best remaining capstan in Purbeck. Nearby are the walls of quarry sheds, called *quarr houses*, and the two *crabstones* that supported a smaller capstan drum. All this, however, is little enough to see on the actual site of a great industry and Swanage council should be encouraged to preserve the Cowlease and it antiquities as a public open space."

The Townsend quarries, I added, were facing a future of quick change - some of the area had been re-dug by open pits, other parts were levelled, and another concealed a caravan camp.

I phoned several Swanage councillors and then followed this up in issue 28 of Dorset County Magazine:

"The last historic relics of underground working in the Purbeck stone trade lie alarmingly close to new housing estates in the old quarrylands above the High Street at Swanage. Industrial archaeologists will have to act immediately to save them for the future. Only two pairs of 'crabstones' survive; these once held wooden capstans to haul carts of stone up from the mine shafts. Donkeys walked around the crabstones in a circular towpath, pulling a lever to turn the capstan. Jeffrey Curtis, who is now in Blackpool, lived in Alexandra Terrace, opposite the quarries on Cowlease Hill, until 1942."

He recalled one of the crabstone pairs still working in Bower's Quarry in 1939:

"I can remember clearly because his donkey was stung by an adder on its face. The quarry just kept on working, it was the last one left above Swanage, but then it suddenly closed. Today, you can still faintly follow round the circle where the donkey used to walk."

Mr Curtis came from a quarrying family and his uncles Ron, Eric and Fred Bower had a modern opencast working above Worth Matravers on the Acton Road. As an occasional visitor to Purbeck, Mr. Curtis warned that these capstan supports - "they are the last two left apart from a couple stuck in a wall in Priest's Road" - were perilously close to the spreading development:

"I reckon the council should take them out and put them in a place where they can be mounted again with a dummy capstan in the middle to show people what they were used for. The quarries themselves will go as all the 'quarr' houses are gone and the shafts have been filled in.

"These crabstones are all that's left of a whole industry that's been going on in Purbeck since the Romans."

There was agreement from David Haysom of Alexandra Terrace, off Cowlease Road, at Swanage. I printed his letter in issue 32 of Dorset County Magazine, in 1973:

"I was most interested to read in Dorset Magazine the account given by Mr. Curtis of the last remaining crabstones that once served the stone industry of Cowlease at Swanage.

"The ones referred to as being at Mr. Bower's quarry are actually standing in the quarry once worked by Mr. C. Benfield more than fifty years ago. This quarry was last worked by Mr. C. Dowland from another shaft facing west, in the same quarry.

"The crabstones at Mr. F. Bower's quarry are partially destroyed and can still be seen above the two shafts. They also worked two 'slides' from one quarry, one going south-west and the other north-west under the new Holbourne Road.

"Two other pairs of crabstones can also be seen within 150 yards of the previously mentioned quarries, one pair once used by Mr. Squibb and later by Mr. W. Brown and Mr. Chinchen, the other pair standing within thirty yards of Manwell Estate and last used by Mr. Joe Norman.

"In Cowlease alone approximately thirty-seven positions of shafts can be traced to this day, Cowlease being the most quarried area in Purbeck.

"Incidentally, with reference to your mention of Cowlease way back in Dorset Magazine issue 12, I have what I am sure is the only model of this quarry in existence. It stands in my garden."

David Haysom wrote a further letter to Dorset County Magazine, which was printed in issue 71 in 1978, recording the destruction of most of the Cowlease workings and pleading for the preservation of the remainder:

"During the past twelve months the majority of the remaining workings have been completely obliterated and replaced by concrete bases for holiday chalets - the crabstones of the old winches having been removed, and the shafts filled to ground level.

"It is unfortunate that Rodney Legg's plea in *Purbeck Island* for the preservation of this unique area was not heeded by the local authorities.

"However, I now write in the hope that something of Swanage's stone industry can still be preserved. For just west of the council caravan site, above Belle Vue Farm (Ordnance Survey map reference SZ 016 782), is what I believe to be the only complete stone quarry remaining in Purbeck. All the quarry houses (with their work benches) are intact, and still surround the towpath. Several retain their stone roofs, and others are covered with rusty corrugated sheeting. The crabstones and their wooden capstan supports remain in position, while the capstan itself (still in good condition) lies in the horses' shed. The entrance to the shaft and its slide - the slope into the underground - also appear excellently preserved, though covered in undergrowth.

"The quarry's survival is largely due to the fact that up to two or three years ago the buildings were used by the landowner for sheltering his cattle, but since then the quarry has been fenced off and nature has taken over completely. The corrugated sheeting on one roof has rusted through and caused a sizable section to collapse. The land on which these workings stand can be of little practical value to the farmer, and I feel strongly that something should be done soon to preserve them before the process of decay takes a firm grip. With a small group of volunteers, perhaps enlisting members of the Langton Preservation Society, it would be possible to clear the undergrowth, repair the buildings, and replace the capstan. This could even be turned into an open air museum of quarrying history, at a bare minimum of financial investment. It has the added advantage of standing beside the area's main public footpath, the Priest's Way."

During my explorations of the Cowlease hillside in 1971, I recorded a second shaft lying west of the spur off Manwell Road and a short distance beyond the buildings. This was a more delicate example of stone mine architecture with the hole having a diameter of twelve feet, its edges carefully rounded and the usual slanting shaft, seven feet six inches wide, projecting outward to the north where the hillside gradually fell away. The top fifteen feet of the shaft could be seen and the rest was filled with earth and rubbish. Its walls were vertical, built upon the bedrock about ten feet below ground level and in a style similar to the drystone walls of Purbeck fields. The first stones were laid upright all round the shaft, except the slide part, and each stone was about twenty inches high and four inches across. On this line, smaller horizontal walling stones, roughly uniform in size, were placed carefully in level layers. The mine entrance was overhung by thick ivy and adjoined by the foundations of small square sheds.

The picture was very different as recently as 1920 when a few lanes were still in use and blocks were tied to low, sturdy carts of elm and hauled by chains to the head of the shaft. Each lane then had its capstan, with a horse providing the power to pull a wooden bar which gave the leverage to turn the drum of the capstan. The bar was called a *spack* and required the horse or mule to plod endlessly along a circular towpath.

The Townsend quarries had the deepest lanes in Purbeck, the largest capstans and the longest spacks. For two hundred years it was the biggest production centre of stone in Purbeck and yet its situation came through simple convenience. Standing above the bay, at the back of Peveril and Durlston, the Cowlease and the other lanes were only yards from Old Swanage and its labour force of quarrymen. Here was the nearest place where stone could be lifted from the ground in workable quantities and they have left the most exhausted ground on the Purbeck limestone.

Lowest of the Purbeck seams to be dug were the *caps* and *new vein*, these two layers being separated by some dirt. At Swanage the caps has been greatly dug and this is the mark of an historic quarrying area. The "old men", when they worked the Townsend, reached all the seams of useable rock: while to the west at Langton Matravers, Acton and Gallows Gore it was exceptional for even two seams to be worked.

Throughout the eighteenth century the stone trade was concentrated at Swanage. Only when business became a struggle, with the danger of over-working the Swanage quarries, did the trade spread west to Langton. Ample stone was then found under the new fields within twenty feet of the surface. There was no longer the need to grope through twelve feet of useless *cinder* in the bowels of the earth to touch the caps. Langton men were busy enough with *freestone* and *downs vein*, and it was in just one place that they ventured to find the real hard stuff below. One of the most scarred hills, near the quarrymen's settlement of Acton, was called Mount Misery, and it overlooked a greener rise in Langton - the latter is still known as Mount Pleasant.

Dr. C. le Neve Foster, inspector of mines for the west of England, carried out a postal survey of the Swanage and Langton quarrylands and reported in 1878:

"The Purbeck stone is a new feature of my statistics. In spite of a great many difficulties, I believe I have at last attained a fairly correct statement of the total amount raised from mines. There are nearly a hundred stone mines in the Swanage district, worked by one, two, or three men underground, who are in many cases the owners as well as the occupiers. Their work is often most irregular; if the men can find work as masons they abandon their quarries for a time, and do not return to them till other work is slack. As the quarrymen of the Isle of Purbeck have never been troubled with Government forms till this year I had considerable difficulty in getting returns from them. Endless mistakes were made, requiring investigation by correspondence, and I may safely say that the ninety-two stone mines near Swanage, employing only 264 persons, gave me more trouble than all the other mines of my district put together. No doubt I shall have much less inconvenience in future years, as the men will soon get into the way of filling up the returns correctly. The following figures represent the number of tons raised during the past year [1877]: Purbeck stone and marble, dressed 11,816 tons 10 cwt. Purbeck stone, undressed - 1,411 tons 10 cwt."

The creation of these quarries came about after 1650 when the mediaeval basis and traditions of the old Purbeck stone and marble trade were finally shattered. Corfe Castle, its castle in ruins, ceased to be its workshop and distribution centre. The ancient track to Ower Quay was abandoned and the trade no longer looked to Poole Harbour as its natural outlet. Instead the first major mines were sunk above the bay at Swanage and cliff quarries started within the next century at Durlston, Tilly Whim and Winspit. By the nineteenth century the coastal quarries extended to Dancing Ledge, Hedbury and Seacombe. The scale of the new operations was vast in comparison with the old and nearly 50,000 tons of stone were shipped from Swanage in some years.

Even in the far-off summers of the old stone trade it was no straightforward task getting worked loads of cut stone from the Townsend quarries to ships standing offshore. The blocks could be handled five times before they were sailing towards the customer. Old Swanage was a quarryman's town and the stone came down the cart tracks to the quarry entrance at Cowlease and was then hauled along the High Street, and through the close-packed lines of cottages at the Narrows to the stacks of stone, called *bankers*, by the shore.

One of the carters from the quarries was injured in an accident in October 1881. The Dorset County Chronicle reported:

"Last week as Mr. Grant's carter, named Pitcher, was coming down the hill from the quarries with three horses and a wagon and about four tons of stone, the tackle for tying up the hind wheel broke and, the weight forcing on the wagon, the carter was knocked down, and the wheels going over both legs broke them. Fortunately the shafts of the wagon striking against the side wall checked and stopped it, or some of the horses might have been killed. The poor carter, in great suffering, is, we hear, progressing but slowly, though, we hope, favourably, under the care and treatment of Dr. G.C. Delamotte. We regret to hear Pitcher is not in any friendly society."

Two weeks later "the poor carter Pitcher" died when "lockjaw set in".

The nineteenth century visitors to Swanage avoided the streets where these stone wagons raised clouds of white, choking dust throughout the best days of summer. Ruts were inches deep and in winter the streets became impassable quagmires of yellow clay. Horses hauled the carts to the quay where each load joined the vast piles of stone and was often later reworked. Sixty loads a day, each of about three tons, came to the water's edge. Many of the bankers stood ten feet high and these giant stacks of stone took up a wide part of the sea front and stretched around the south-east of the town from the Royal Victoria Hotel along to the White House.

C.E. Robinson described the bankers in his book published in 1882, *A Royal Warren: Picturesque Rambles in the Isle of Purbeck*. His foresight was lacking somewhat for although the bankers have vanished they were replaced by bricks and mortar and not the seafront pleasure gardens that he visualised. Swanage in the early 1880s was still very much a town of the stone trade:

"... its unsightly wharves, piled high with stone, which extend some hundred yards along the curve of the bay, directly in front of the principal terrace, and excluding all view of the sea from anyone walking on the pavement.

"Here, on raised platforms intersected by wagon-roads, are stored the wrought stones of every kind, which have been carted down to the merchants from the quarries on the hill where they were dug, and here they remain until the day of shipment; when a cargo hurriedly leaves the bankers, only to be replaced by newly-collected loads. Even more destructive of the amenities of Swanage as a watering place than its narrow inconvenient old streets, are these bankers occupying and disfiguring as they do the very spot where pretty gardens, with broad gravelly paths, should be laid out as a public seaside promenade.

"Hitherto the requirements of the staple trade of the place, the 'chipping and shipping of stone', as it has been aptly termed, have almost necessitated this consecration to unlovely trade; but there is some hope now that the coming railway will lead to the transport of the stone instead of by ship, and set the bankers free."

The dependence upon boats to take the stone from the bankers out to the ships anchored in Swanage Bay gave the stone trade a shaky system of exportation. That it lasted so long, and only ceased after the arrival of the railway, is to some extent a reflection on the appalling condition of Purbeck roads. The first turnpike of 1768 was little improvement over the mediaeval road pattern as it went from Stoborough to Creech Grange and then linked with rough older roads to climb the ridge at Bare Cross and approach Corfe from the west. It did not even extend to Swanage.

A proper carriage road followed a little later, running directly across the heath to Corfe and then through Kingston and Langton to Swanage, bringing the port into direct contact with inland Dorset for the first time. The toll houses and gates were at the north end of Stoborough village and at Swanage, opposite Jubilee Road, on the High Street, Herston. Another apparently existed at Gallows Gore, although it has left no official record, but the main building there was formerly called Turnpike Cottages.

The course of the present A351 between Corfe and Herston did not become a through road until after 1862: it would inevitably have been utilised eventually by the stone trade but the railway's coming in 1885 had far more immediate and decisive effects. Had that arrived later then the steam traction engine might have provided an alternative for heavy haulage. The point, however, is that the operation of the Swanage stone boats up to a hundred years ago was not an outmoded custom from the past but because they were still an effective working system. So the bankers survived until the turn of the twentieth century.

In those days, when buyers had been found and ships were waiting to take the stone, the blocks were loaded into high-wheeled stone carts. These waited at the bankers, were drawn by horses down to the beach and into the sea, and then the stone was transferred into boats. The stone barges plied between the wading carts and ships standing further out in the bay.

Purpose built and pointed at stem and stern, so they did not have to be turned around, the barges were cumbersome boats but they carried immense stones, some weighing half a ton. Manned by two men with oars, the boats also had a small lug-sail for when the wind was favourable. They ferried a load of six to nine tons on each journey. The stone was shipped differently from Durlston Bay. Here the stone boats were hauled close inshore and an inclined stage placed nearby. The blocks of stone were then slid down the ramp and lowered into the waiting boat, helped along by quarrymen who often stood waist-deep in the sea for hours.

As well as taking stone out, the barges were also used as a lifeline into the town. They brought ashore coal and other supplies from coasters anchored in the bay. At the middle of the nineteenth century there was an average of seventy stone craft operating at Swanage and in an easterly gale and during the hardest weather all boats were hauled ashore and safely grounded. It was a wet and tricky job, only possible by using capstans rollers and chains, but a vital one because the barges would otherwise soon be overwhelmed and sink. The boats were also vulnerable to accidents, especially when meeting the cross-currents as they rounded the ledges of Peveril Point while bringing stone from Durlston to Swanage Bay. One such sad case happened there in August 1836 when young John Norman drowned after the sea swamped his father's craft. The following day he was to have been married.

The sight of tall carts being pulled by horses into the sea, out to the waiting barges, was not the only remarkable scene in Swanage during the first half of the last century. During the early 1800s the town was still using its own currency which was based on the ancient system of barter. Emanating from the Townsend quarries, the almost unbelievable fact is that it came in units of 12 lb. and 144 lb. in weight.

Coins that were pieces of stone were issued as quarrymen's wages and then traded across the counters of shops in the same way as the current legal tender, King George pennies. Tradesmen's counters had also to be slabs of stone in order to withstand rough treatment from the "Swanage pennies" which were shaped like paving stone. Twelve pennies equalled, logically enough, one shilling and that was the second unit of the quarried currency, weighing as near 144 lb. as possible.

Although this was a form of barter, the shopkeepers handled the stone as a direct fixed-price equivalent of the normal bronze coins and their counters were known as bankers, like the piles of stone on the seafront. Even the official pennies of the time were huge if compared with our late pre-decimalisation pennies and those outsized pieces of copper have themselves been abandoned.

Some Swanage traders did resist payments in stone, but only when they had a delicate business in such small items as snuff, pepper, vinegar and salt - and had a woman on the other side of the counter. William Masters Hardy remembered the Swanage pennies and wrote the following at the turn of the twentieth century:

"I have seen quarrymen carrying stones on their backs from the quarries to pay for their beer, baccy, and other commodities. Land, coals, bread, boots, clothes and almost every article required for home consumption could be bought with stone currency."

Bowler hats are no longer worn by the quarrymen and moleskin trousers were discarded as opencast workings replaced the underground mines. Moleskin trousers are remembered by the old men who wore them as "fine things for underground" but they can also recall the surprising heaviness of their clothes after being caught above ground by a sudden downpour. Made not from the skins of moles, but from a strong cotton fustian, the pile of which is shaved, the trousers lasted for years. They can withstand much rough treatment and are still worn by foundry workers to protect their legs from sparks. Fustian (called *fuskin* in Purbeck) can be washed but never dry-cleaned, though it was always considered better just to leave it alone. Moleskins were a sort of baggy leggings of brownish-white thick cloth, and when worn to shape the trousers were usually hung "at ease" ready to be stepped into.

Nelson Thomson, one of the older quarrymen living and working at Acton, used to have moleskins and can also remember when the quarrymen were still wearing their traditional bowler hats:

"When they built the sea wall down at Swanage in 1904, there's quite a lot of those men then [he pointed to a photograph] wearing a real hard bowler hat. You could take one and play football with it. I could remember my father wearing one on special days and I could go back to the early 1920s and there was quite a lot of the old men still wearing them. We did have a bowler hat dug up from one of the quarries up here when one of the men got out [after an accident underground] and never got hurted. But he did leave a bowler hat down there and later we went and touched it; it all fell to pieces. That was up here on top, opposite Gallows Gore, back in the 1920s.

"I used to work with a man named Billy Brown back in 1922 and he used to wear a bowler hat. He used to go to church and Wareham market and wear his bowler hat. Billy Brown was living down in Langton village and he used to work up at the cliff quarries. He was nearly eighty when he died and he bin dead nearly forty years. I went into the stone trade in 1925. I had to pay £5 7s 6d and a penny loaf and a quart of beer. Real tasty job in those days. In the little village hall at Corfe, and I had to go down and kick the ball up through Aves [The Halves], as they do call it. I was the last one to be married into the trade and I had to kick the football - the last place to kick the ball, the villagers could go and pick en up and take en away. That was the quarryman's right for that day ..."

Such ancient rights were the subject of a report by the government's inspector of factories and workshops, issued in March 1880. This was reported in the Globe newspaper and referred to the "islanders" of Purbeck and Portland as remarkable in their habits and having "a settled idea that the workings of the quarries in those localities is a privilege of their own, and they not only resent the intrusion of other workmen but go so far as to qualify the latter and, indeed, the whole world outside Purbeck and Portland, by the opprobrious title of 'foreigners'. The Purbeckians of Swanage maintain that this privilege is secured to them by an ancient charter providing that no person may establish himself in their trade who is not a direct descendant of some local quarryman.

"This, however, is far from being the whole extent of the immunities claimed by the islanders ... Both peoples have a strong objection to being interfered with, the Purbeckians especially holding a sort of tradition that they are beyond all laws, and that they would have a sort of right to make regulations for their own government, the general sum of which appears to be to arrange that they should do as much, or as little, work as they please, have unlimited beer, and send their offspring to school, or not, at discretion, which would result in about ninety per cent growing up uneducated as their parents boast that they are themselves.

"So tenacious are both races of their individuality that they will not even contract matrimonial alliances with the foreigner, but intermarry amongst themselves so that nearly everybody in both localities is related to everybody else. Notwithstanding this fact, it appears that the evils which are generally supposed to result from intermarriage are not particularly noticeable but, on the contrary, the health of the community is so good that no one could fail to be struck by their unusually fine appearance, and at Portland boys of thirteen or fourteen are often found to look as if they were two years older."

In a court case in 1880 it was heard that a young boy, Jesse Stickland, was working full-time stone dressing at Swanage and had not been sent to school. In his father's defence, it was said that Swanage quarrymen were under the impression that "lads working in the mines do not cone under the Elementary Education Act. They thought the inspector was carrying out the spirit of an obnoxious act which was hostile to them. They think that they can do what they like with their own children."

The case was found to be proved but no fine was imposed. me magistrates only "wished the defendants to comply with the law of the country" and ordered payment of costs. It was pointed out by the inspector that the stone workers could send their children to work at ten-years-old, providing they kept them at school half-time until they were thirteen. George Burt, one of the justices, remarked that Purbeck men were rather strong headed but he would advise them to look upon the inspector as a friend rather than an enemy. The inspector replied: "We are on the best terms except when it comes to keeping the law!"

The Earl of Eldon supported the backlash against the Act and was in the chair at a meeting of the Wareham and Purbeck Union which came out in favour of ending "the compulsory sending to school by the labouring and industrial classes of children after the age of twelve, and allowing their full employment at that age".

The Langton Matravers burial registers show that several children met horrible deaths in the depths of the more confined mines. One old quarryman told a Swanage historian, John T. Dean: " They wuss cheap, plenny of 'em and more wur they come vrom."

It was a Dorsetman, W.E. Forster of Bradpole near Bridport, who had given birth to the monster that is now state education. For us at this point in time it is becoming increasingly difficult to understand the nature and extent of the child labour problem - and harder to accept the fact that ten-year-old boys were working a man's hours at a man's job in the stone mines of Swanage.

Purbeck also provides an example of industrial trade restrictions in action in the 1860s. Four lads were thrown out of work in the quarries because the operatives' trade union, the Company of Marblers and Stonecutters, disapproved of their employment - because they thought it deprived their own members of jobs. The youngsters were regarded as cheap alternative labour.

Nathan Chinchin White is the signatory, and it is witnessed by two wardens of the company, Richard Benfield and another of more difficult signature. The document is dated in Swanage, 29 March 1865:

"I do hereby agree with the wardens of the Company of Marblers and Stonecutters of the Isle of Purbeck, to discharge from my employ on Saturday April 1st 1865 two lads viz Dowland and Cole. I further agree to discharge from my employ in June 1865 one lad viz Damon. I also further agree to discharge from my employ of June 1866 one lad viz Milehall. Frederick Arney to continue in my employ but not to become a member of the Company. I also further agree not to employ any more lads contrary to the wish of the said Company of Marblers and Stonecutters."

This agreement, which carries a sixpenny fiscal stamp, was discovered by Peter Hill and reported in issue 90 of Dorset County Magazine.

It is far from easy to envisage how a Purbeck mine shaft must have looked. These openings in the ground were sometimes more than mere work holes. Several of those around Langton and Acton were used until 1930 as sources of fresh water for the cottages. Men and women queued for their turn to climb down twenty feet with a bucket. John Dean was told by a quarryman that the stone and underpicking dirts provided quick filter beds: "Feller cud'ave a crap anner piss one wick. Tu, three wicks later ee'd draw it up from th'well, all viltered and reel sweet."

The old shafts are still there, though mainly stopped up at the entrance, and one was reopened at Webber's quarry and found to have air so foul that a candle would no longer burn there. Experiences such as these belong to an era that has vanished. There are still some quarrymen who remember cutting stone from holes in the ground and they know that the depth of an old shaft could have been gauged by the size of its capstan.

Langton's capstans were quite small to tackle the shallow workings, and unlike those at Swanage Townsend, could be worked by a donkey harnessed to the spack. An old pony could wind a ton up the quarry shaft as it walked at the end of a sixteen-foot spack round a six-foot capstan of elm. Such an arrangement was said to raise a ton by six feet every time the animal went round. When a cart and its stone was lifted to the top of the slide, the pony would then be unharnessed from the spack and attached directly to the cart to pull the stone to the working floor. The usual place for the horse or donkey shed was beside the towpath, and adjoining the opening of the mine shaft. A capstan was a tough piece of machinery and only required an occasional greasing of the gudgeon. It would last a human lifetime and wear out several old mules in the process.

If a horse was not available, manpower could be used instead. Even as late as about 1850, two Swanage girls had to tread the spack, "as their father was an old man and had no one to help him, his daughters were compelled to walk round and round in the mud and clay up to their ankles".

Throughout the twentieth century the capstans rotted and there was only that one at Cowlease with all its stone intact, matched by a second just south of Belle Vue Farm at Herston, but I have frequently found pairs of crabstones still standing. These supported the capstan drum and a hole at the top, through the sides of both stones, shows where a beam held the axle in place.

RAF Hospital - established towards the end of the Great War for convalescent cases. Captain Clement Perronet Sells of the Royal Army Medical Corps "died on July 4th 1919 at R.A.F. Hospital Swanage, of illness contracted on Active Service, Aged 29 years".

He is buried in Northbrook Road Cemetery. A nearby stone is to Flight-Lieutenant P.L.T. Lewin of the RAF who died on 9 September 1919.

Lieutenant-Colonel Leslie Jenkins from Swanage, serving with the Royal Flying Corps and then the RAF, was killed in the Great War.

Ragged Rocks - long line of jagged offshore rocks immediately beneath the cliff-face of Round Down, extending half-a-mile eastwards from Belle Vue Cliffs (Ordnance Survey map reference SZ 020 768) virtually to Anvil Point (SZ 028 768).

They claimed the horrific shipwreck of the *Alexandrovna* [*see her entry*] in 1882.

Railway - an offshoot of the London and South Western Railway, a single-track branch line built in 1885, ran from Wareham to Swanage via an intermediate station at Corfe Castle. Though the line escaped the Richard Beeching axe it lingered only until 1972 and with its closure the track onward from Furzebrook to the seaside was lifted.

This stimulated a spirited campaign for its revival with the Swanage Railway Society securing a lease of the line from Dorset County Council and relaying a mile of track to Herston in the early 1980s and pushing on to Corfe and beyond a decade later.

It was a struggle to get the railway into Purbeck, to try and keep it there, and then followed a quarter of a century of campaigning, fund raising and physical hard graft to replace the track that British Rail raised with such indecent haste.

Originally, the line was seen as an industrial railway for the stone trade.

George Edmund Street, the architect who built the Law Courts in the Strand and a second church at Kingston, south of Corfe Castle, told a colleague about his use of the *burr*, Purbeck's building stone, and added:

"Let the rail or tram go to where that stone is, put it on the rail at once, and I will undertake that six churches out of seven shall be built with that material."

George Burt took up the cause of bringing the railway to strengthen the commercial potential of Purbeck. He held meetings to push forward the idea that the railway's coming was inevitable. He repeated Street's views and said:

"Swanage has been a place of stone for many years, but the great place now is a little to the west where there is an immense quantity of stone that could be carried to a profitable market if only they would lessen the cost of carriage. If Swanage is to move ahead and you are get out of the dirty streets into a more wholesome and profitable atmosphere, you must have a railway."

Railway engineers surveyed Purbeck in 1880, and the following year, despite opposition from Wareham, an act was finally passed for the second time to enable the building of a railway to Swanage. There was no objection from the Earl of Eldon who owned much of the land across which the line was to run. Capital of £90,000 was authorised for the project and work started on 5 May 1883 at Wareham. Ten miles further on, with the date 5 May 1885, the line was completed. A year later, the Swanage branch was bought by the London and South Western Railway and the town became a holiday resort. There was a scheme for a 1,338 yard spur to connect Swanage station with the stone *bankers* and tramway leading to the old pier, but no progress with this was made.

From the time the railway opened the seafront stone trade was doomed and it would die by 1896. The bankers were still piled with stone in 1880 but by the turn of the century the Parade and Institute Road had risen from their remains. Seaborne trade from Swanage ceased in the 1890s and one last stone barge retired to Chapman's Pool where it rotted. Burt's stone-weighing office is now a travel agency.

Instead of carrying stone - though the Furzebrook end still carries ball clay and now oil - the seaside end of the Purbeck branch line became a scenic holiday railway. Its special work-horses were the M7 0-4-4 tank engines, which ran a push-and-pull shuttle between Wareham and Swanage. They were withdrawn in 1964 and for a couple of years the line had an interesting assortment of steam locomotives that were seconded to Purbeck whilst waiting their turn to be scrapped.

From 1966 the line was worked by diesel multiple units, each of three cars, and had a particularly busy summer in 1969 as closure threatened. Public demand caused through trains to be resumed to Waterloo on summer Saturdays, the hotel and boarding-house changeover day, and were packed with hundreds of passengers. Seven of these trains to London are shown in one of the last timetables; each was of nine or ten coaches.

After closure there was still hope but the cruel reality of the removal of the track made the revival of the Purbeck branch seem to many of us like yet another Dorset lost cause. We counted without the energy of Andrew Goltz who had the vision not only to talk Dorset County Council into leasing his preservation society the station at Swanage, and then the line itself, but almost succeeded in bringing home the town's named mainline locomotive as their flagship [see the entry for 'Swanage'].

As something of a light-weight consolation prize, Goltz instead brought to his group's Swanage base - appropriately, the railway station - a small petrol-driven shunting engine called *Beryl*. She worked the coal sidings of Coralls at Hamworthy and was bought by two Poole men, Geoff Pitman and John Vickery.

One vintage exhibit also returned to the Purbeck line. It was a wheel-less coach body, thirty-four feet long with six compartments, which was found at Highcliffe, Christchurch, where it had been since 1921. It is thought to have been made about 1885 and is now resting beside the old cattle pen at Corfe Castle station. The carriage has been repainted in its original London and South Western Railway livery of dark brown and salmon pink.

Despite the *Swanage* setback, the group did not abandon its attempts to bring an ex-British Railways steam locomotive to Purbeck from Barry scrapyard in South Wales. Their second choice, a standard Class-4 engine numbered 80078, was paid for amidst acrimony about "ill treatment by rival societies".

The group brought 80078 by road "to safety" at Swanage in 1976. She was built in 1953 and worked until 1962 from Stratford on the Southend commuter services. With electrification of the Essex lines she was moved to North Wales and went to Barry after being sold for scrap in 1968.

80078 was saved through the efforts of Noel McManus, who had shown me over her at Barry in 1973:

"Fortunately for us she was reboiled in the 1960s, and we've a full report from an ex-BR Swindon man who estimates it will cost £700 to get it going again. It's an engine that's easy to steam and an economical runner - that's why we chose it.

"We have come here and poured gallons of oil over it every weekend for months. This loosens up the parts for when we have to strip it down, and also soaks in to fight the rust."

Vandalism was a problem at Barry, but not so much from Welsh youth as from other railway fanatics:

"People are fighting dirty and there is absolutely no respect. Other societies are removing bits and robbing parts from the engines that are already being saved. We have lost the firebox door and lubricators ad infinitum. They let you do the hard work of easing the parts and then come along and take them. The stupid thing is that they don't need them. They've got engines like this themselves and want to put aside some spares to save them paying casting expenses in the future."

There were to be more arrivals. The Great Western Steam Preservation Group selected an 0-6-2 tank engine designed by Charles Collett, of the 56xx class, from the rusting collection at Barry. She had been built by Armstrong Whitworth at Newcastle in 1928 and spent her whole career working from Swansea, being withdrawn from service in July 1964.

Her purchase fund ran out of steam but a local supporter then came to her rescue and enabled £4,500 to be paid to Woodham Bros., owners of Barry Dock scrapyard, in 1978. The engine was loaded on to the trailer of D.J. Hedgeman Ltd, from Wool, on 13 May 1979 and brought to Swanage. She arrived just before noon on the 15th, minus nine inches of chimney which had to be cut off to get her under the motorway bridges. A replacement chimney, in better condition and complete with a copper cap, was purchased later. 6695 has been painted in the British Railways' lined-green livery of her middle age and given the appropriate Landore shed plate (number 87E), as that was her home from 1948 to 1960.

For practical purposes, whilst the steam engines were being renovated, the railway's operations have relied on former industrial diesel locomotives, such as the thirty-ton 421-class engine produced by John Fowler and Company at Leeds in 1957, works number 4210132. She had led an inexhausting life on military reserve fuel depots around Manchester until her arrival at Swanage in 1978 ended the pension on the state. She took on most of the hard work at Swanage, as Geoff Pitman pointed out, and enabled the revival of the first mile of the Purbeck line, relaid to Herston. Another moment of relief was when the railway's smaller diesel,

Richard Trevithick, passed her boiler inspection. Built in 1954, to a design by Andrew Barclay, she had worked at Goldrington power station, Bedford.

The pride and joy of the Southern Steam Trust volunteers at Swanage is a class T9 4-4-0 Victorian locomotive which is the epitome of steam nostalgia in both age and looks. Built at Nine Elms - now the new Covent Garden - in 1899, engine No.120 of the London and South Western Railway is the survivor of sixty-six "Greyhounds" built by Dugald Drummond. Train enthusiast Gerald Nabarro used to describe them as Drummond's masterpiece of grace and reliability. No.120 has the distinctive early railways flourish of great rounded housings over the forward pair of big wheels, a characteristic Eastleigh smoke-stack widening towards the top, and an eight-wheeled tender.

She is a splendid beast and reason enough for visiting Swanage, preferably as part of a working railway rather than as a static exhibit. Extending the line to Herston, Harman's Cross, Corfe Castle and Norden, has coincided with a colossal prospective obstacle being removed. Each stage of its expansion, towards the objective of restoration of the link with British Rail mainline services at Wareham, had to be examined before granting of a "Light Railway Order", but at Corfe a bigger problem loomed.

In May 1992, the National Trust announced that it had withdrawn its objection to the extension of the railway to a terminus north of Corfe, following undertakings received from Dorset County Council and Purbeck District Council:

"The Trust had been concerned that extension of the railway might prejudice its preferred option for a future Corfe bypass. The authorities insist that this route, which runs beside the railway, will be fully protected and that car-parking in Corfe will be safeguarded from traffic generated by the railway."

The rebirth of the railway has been something unique and admirable that Swanage is contributing to Dorset. Townspeople such as Jack Hardy and Mike Northover have made sacrifices to keep progress on line, encouraged by the camaraderie of the volunteer work-force on the ground. All believe that a tourist county such as Dorset must be able to support one steam railway to what is one of the most highly visited pieces of coastline in Britain. The line's viability and future will be ensured the day that the first steam train since 1966 is able to take passengers the full ten miles back up the line from Swanage to Wareham Station.

In 1994 the Swanage collection of steam locomotives comprised:

4-4-0 Class T9.
British Railways No. 30120.
Built at Nine Elms in 1899, being engine No. 120 of the London and South Western Railway.
On loan. In store, pending awaiting arrangements for overhaul, to be agreed with the National Railway Museum.

4-6-2 Battle of Britain Class.
No. 34072, *257 (Burma) Squadron*.
Built at Brighton in 1948 for Southern Region of British Railways.
Ex-Barry Dock scrapyard. Overhauled 1989.

4-6-2 Merchant Navy Class.
No. 35022, *Holland-America Line*.
Built at Eastleigh in 1948 for Southern Region of British Railways.
Ex-Barry Dock scrapyard.
In store, awaiting move to Herston Works for restoration.

2-6-4T British Railways Standard Class 4MT.
No. 80078.
Built at Brighton in 1954.
Ex-Barry Dock scrapyard, due for next-stage restoration in the Herston works; "several major parts are subject to quotation".

2-6-4T British Railways Standard Class 4MT.
No. 80104.
Built at Brighton in 1955.
Ex-Barry Dock scrapyard, currently being restored at Bitton on the Avon Valley Railway.

2-8-0 Class 8F, "Turkish Stanier".
No. 45160.
Being restored at Hamworthy.

0-4-0T Hunslet tank engine.
No. 1684.
Formerly nicknamed *Sad Sam* but now regarded as a friend of *Thomas the Tank Engine*. In store awaiting overhaul.

0-4-4T Class M7.
No. 30053.
Built for the London and South Western Railway. Subject to a running agreement made by Swanage Railway Society, 1993-98, with outings booked to other railways.

0-6-0T.
No. 47160, *Cunarder*.
Spent summer 1993 on the Lavender Line in Sussex.
Returned for the Swanage Railway's autumn gala on 14 September 1993.
Fitted with steam heating equipment during winter 1993-94.

0-6-0T Class 1F.
No. 41712 (previously numbered 41708).
Ex-Midland Railway. Overhauled in 1993 but still requiring "a new right-hand clack valve assembly".
Booked for visits to the Dean Forest Railway and Midland Railway Trust. Its "boiler certificate" for 1984-94, enabling public use, expires in October - so she will require an overhaul in 1995.

0-6-0T Yogoslavian USA "Yankee Tank" Class.
No. 30075.
Given a boiler examination, overhauled brake cylinders, and re-adjusted compound springing in 1993.

0-6-2T Great Western Railway Class 5600.
No. 6695.
Built by Armstrong Whitworth in 1928.
Candidate for restoration in the newly completed Herston Works.

0-6-0ST Austerity Class.
Joseph.
In store. Owned by Touche Ross (from the closed Chatterly Whitfield Mining Museum, Stoke-on-Trent).

0-6-0ST Peckett Class.
No. 2150.
In store. Offered for sale (requiring restoration).

Ramsbottom - commercial educationalist **John William Ramsbottom** [1883-1966] lived at The Bushes, Durlston, Swanage. He was director of the City of London College [1925-45] and then one of its governors [1945-56], and a committee member of numerous organisations involved in industrial education. He is buried in Swanage Cemetery, Washpond Lane, Godlingston.

Redhorn Quay - one of the oldest ferry services in Dorset connected eastern Purbeck with the port of Poole. The service for Swanage and Studland ran from Redhorn Quay in Poole Harbour, on the west side of the South Haven Peninsula (Ordnance Survey map reference SZ 022 855). This quay has the remains of *bankers* of stone that show it was once, like Ower, used by the Purbeck stone trade.

The quay at Redhorn was described for me by Ben Pond:

"It is composed of huge, square-cut stone, tier upon tier, with deep water alongside. Fifty odd years ago there were deep wheel ruts leading across to the quay. Slowly, Redhorn Channel has silted at its entrance, from South Deep, since 1922."

Other stones, found in the mud of the harbour shore and especially near Goathorn, include granite boulders. These do not have local origins but were brought as ballast by ships that entered Poole Harbour to collect stone, marble and clay.

Robinson - art connoisseur **Sir (John) Charles Robinson** [1824-1913], Director of the Victoria and Albert Museum [1852-69] produced numerous publications for the South Kensington Museum, as the institution was then known. He lived at Newton Manor, Swanage (*see its entry*) and embellished its seventeenth century rooms with Italian and other European fittings. These include doors, a staircase, shields, carved friezes dated to 1656-58, and a flying-fish weather vane which is said to have come from Billingsgate Market.

Sir Charles was a frequent contributor to the arts columns of The Times and the Nineteenth Century Review.

His eldest son, **Charles Robinson** [1853-1913], who died the same year as his father, published *Picturesque Rambles in the Isle of Purbeck* in 1882. He also wrote the *Cruise of the 'Widgeon'* [1876] and several collections of poems.

This Charles was a barrister. He adopted the Swanage house name to distinguish himself from his father and in later life was known as Charles Edmund Newton-Robinson. He collected engraved gems, was an accomplished yacht racer, and sword-fenced for Britain in the Athens Olympics of 1906.

The Rookery - see entry for **Seymer Road**

Round Down Signal Station - a Royal Navy signal station was in operation to the south of Swanage during the Napoleonic wars, on Round Down (Ordnance Survey map reference SZ 025 771) 1,500 feet north-west of the present Anvil Point Lighthouse. It relayed shore to ship naval signals by telegraph, on the system revised by Sir Home Riggs Popham [1762-1820] and then by semaphore using a great upright hoarding of circles and squares like an oversize cricket scoreboard. The foundations of a walled enclosure on Round Down, with six ancillary buildings, can be traced. They are grouped around a depression about eighteen feet by twenty feet that marks the site of the signals apparatus.

Royal Victoria Hotel - originally the Manor house erected by Thomas Chapman [1664]. Its transformation into the rather grand Manor House

Hotel was carried out by philanthropist William Morton Pitt, as his last major endeavour, at the age of seventy-one [1825-27]. Pitt added two wings and a stable-block, parts of which survive at the heart of the present building. The name changed from the Manor House to the Victoria Hotel after Princess Victoria and her mother, the Duchess of York, spent a night there [August 1833; not the later date given by the editors of the third edition of John Hutchins's county history] between visiting Corfe Castle and sailing to the Isle of Wight.

After Pitt's death [1836] it was sold at auction, being the second of his estate's thirty-nine lots [1838] and described as the "well-known celebrated hotel at Swanage" containing "every convenience and accommodation which can be required". There was "a lawn, fenced with iron rails, in the front, capital gardens and yards attached, and between the front of the hotel and the sea is a private pier or quay handsomely built and finished as a place of embarking and landing, whilst it forms a marine promenade for the visitors".

The new owners added "Royal" to the name and the next visitor of that line was Albert Edward, Prince of Wales - heir to the throne as his mother had been when she was in Swanage - on a walking tour at the age of fifteen [26 September 1856]. He had come from Wimborne and had two escorts. Travelling incognito, the party requested three beds, but had to play the royal card to get the third after the landlord said he had only two available and that "the young gentleman must put up with a sofa in the corridor". Next day they walked along the cliffs to St Alban's Head.

Standards fit for royalty were upheld in Queen Victoria's last decade by Miss Isabella Vincent [1891]. She ran a tight ship for staff and guests alike until a few years after the Great War [1923].

It ceased to be an hotel after suffering the down-market spectacle of stallholders regularly infesting the elegant lawns [1972]. Next owner Ray Beck converted it to flats [1978].

Rüdesheim - an attractive wine-town on the Rhine, in Germany, with which Swanage is twinned [since 1985].

St Mark's Church - in Bell Street, Herston, this simple Victorian building has a steeply pitched roof with a bell-turret. It is an Anglican church and the "MDCCCLXIX" on the foundation stone coincided with the demise of its architect, John Hicks of Dorchester, who died on 12 February 1869.

The work was brought to a conclusion by George Crickmay of Weymouth, almost certainly through his assistant Thomas Hardy, the novelist. Hardy had been Hicks's pupil [1856-62] and was employed by him again towards the end of the decade [1867-69]. On Hicks's death, Crickmay took on Hardy specifically to finish off the church projects that he had inherited from Hicks.

Shortage of money delayed completion and consecration of the Herston church until 25 April 1872; St Mark's day. The master mason was Felix G. Fooks of Herston and the style was described at the time as "a plain Early English village church, inexpensive" - at £1,400 - "but nevertheless pretty and of effective design".

Its oldest feature is secondhand, being an octagonal 1663-dated Purbeck stone font from St Mary's Church. The building was extended at the south-west corner in the 1970s.

St Mary's Church - the Anglican parish church, beside the mill-pond in the heart of the old town, with only the fifteenth century tower surviving from the mediaeval building.

This tower is a puzzle. It has walls that are nearly five feet in thickness and is built without ornamentation, almost as if it was intended to double as fort or at least a secure refuge. In this context the church's position may also be relevant. It is above the Brook, which has its only un-culverted section in the next-door grounds of Swanwic House, but it has to be remembered that this was formerly a wide, tidal backwater. The lowest downstream crossing point, from Northbrook Road, was here, opposite the parish church. Not that this proves it had any strategic purpose, as for the attending of services and bringing burials it would obviously have been sensible for the church to be located in a position also accessible from the northern half of the parish.

Victorian and Edwardian rebuildings were almost total, with the former of 1859-60 being represented by the nave, south transept and stair-turret, and the 1907-08 expansion extends northwards into what is in effect a second church running parallel to the Victorian building and stretching further west than the tower.

The Victorian architect was Thomas Henry Wyatt [1807-80] whose major works include the Liverpool Exchange, Wilton Church, Knightsbridge Barracks and the Athenaeum extensions. As consultant architect to the Incorporated Church Building Society and Salisbury Diocesan Society he designed or restored a total of more than 150 churches. His idiom for Swanage was thirteenth century gothic.

Perpendicular styles of the fifteenth century were chosen by architects J.E. Clifton and E.A. Robinson, both of Swanage. Their work has its stone on the north-east outside corner, dated 10 October 1907, laid by Winifred Parsons, daughter of rector Rev W.H. Parsons. The builders, also from the town, were H. and J. Hardy and the principal mason was Isaac Edmonds.

An ancient consecration cross, discovered during the rebuilding, was "built into the north wall of the new nave on the inside". Other earlier features include thirteenth century moulded fragments, two fourteenth century coffin-lids, and the remains of a couple of fifteenth century cusped window-heads.

Safari - the wreck of **HMS** *Safari*, a Second World War submarine, lies off Anvil Point, Swanage. She would claim the life of Poole lifeboatman Pete Benson [July 1992] whose second-hand buoyancy gear failed him on a dive.

Sandwich - old name for Swanage, see entry for **Swanwich**

Sentry Road - named for Sentry Field, between Seymer Road and Park Road to the west of Peveril Downs, with its military tag dating long before its early nineteenth century use as a coastal observation post. It then became the Watch and Preventive Station and was part of the estate of William Morton Pitt until his 1836 bankruptcy.

Seymer Road - facing Peveril Downs is a graceful Regency terrace built for William Morton Pitt [1828] with three-storey stucco and slate Belvedere House (postcode BH19 2AL) at the top end, graced by a wrought-iron balcony. Built originally as three houses, they are now two with the northern part being known as Belvedere Lodge (also BH19 2AL).

Another building of note, originally the Custom House of the 1830s, is Rookery Court, now The Rookery (BH19 2AQ) which did have rooks until the last row of tall elms was felled [1898]. John Dampier had planted most of the trees, prior to Pitt's arrival [1823].

Seymer Road was named for Grace Seymer, Pitt's second wife.

Shell Bay overhead cable-cars plan - the final scheme by the Burt family of Swanage for improving Purbeck's communications, revealed in 1904, was killed by small-town politics at Poole and Bournemouth. The ambitious idea was to convey tramcars across the water between Sandbanks and Shell Bay by means of overhead cables. Others suggested a suspension bridge instead. The Bournemouth Graphic reported:

"We are enabled to publish this week the official announcement that the plans and arrangements for an important development of the tramway system to Canford Cliffs and Swanage are practically complete. This is the first announcement that has been made on the matter, and we are in a position to give authentic details of the scheme in so far as present arrangements permit.

"A private company has been formed, and among those taking a prominent part in its working, we believe, are Sir John Burt, of Swanage, and Mr. Bankes, of Corfe Castle, to establish a system of trams, which will start from the Westbourne Arcade, and run through Seamoor Road and Branksome Park, across Canford Cliffs to Sandbanks. Here it is proposed to erect a tower on either side of the water, and by means of a cage and chain arrangement to swing the cars across to the opposite bank and thence continue the system to Swanage. We understand that it has not yet been decided whether the line of route will pass through Studland, though the whole scheme is complete in all but one or two minor details.

"The capital of the company is to be £68,000, and we are informed that practically the whole of this sum has already been privately subscribed. No appeal will therefore be made to the public."

Shipwrecks - see entries for **HMS** *Abel Tasman*, *Alexandrovna*, *Annie Margretta*, *Brodick Castle*, *Constitution*, **Danish Fleet**, *Fanny*, *Forest*

Queen, *Jean-Marie*, *Kyarra*, *Neptune*, *HMS Safari*, *Sisters*, **Spanish Wreck**, and *Wild Wave*.

Sisters - Exeter schooner wrecked on the ledges off Peveril Point [November 1827] with the loss of seven of her crew. One man was rescued, dragged ashore at great risk to themselves by a party of Swanage Coast Guards and boatmen who were rewarded by the newly formed Royal National Institution for the Preservation of Lives from Shipwreck, founded by Sir William Hillary [1824].

Spanish wreck - name unknown, off Swanage in 1425, not documented in English records.

Springs bubbling off Swanage and Studland - the water seeping more than eighty feet below Ulwell, at the south-east end of Ballard Down, is lost as far as abstraction methods are concerned. It runs into a fault which drains the side of Ballard Down in an eastward direction and issues from the seabed between the north end of Swanage beach and the headland at the end of the down. Fresh water bubbles up in quantity and the flow continued through the 1976 drought. A century before the bargemen carrying stone from Swanage knew the spot, and lowered casks into the sea to fill them with drinking water. A similar location where fishermen used to drink is known in Kimmeridge Bay.

Richard Gough's second edition of John Hutchins's *History of Dorset* records a similar series of underwater springs:

"On the south side of the Studland Bay, near Handfast Point or Old Harry, are three springs of fresh water, twelve feet below high water mark: the largest of which discharges between four and five tons of water in a minute. They are within ten feet of each other and run in parallel courses."

"Stewpot" - disc-jockey Ed Stewart, full name **Edward Stewart Mainwaring** [born 1941], the son of Mr and Mrs Ray Mainwaring of South Barn, South Cliff Road, has been a frequent visitor to Swanage. Not that he is quite native, having been born when his mother was evacuated from London to Devon. His father, a Treasury solicitor, retired to Swanage and became a town councillor.

Straw Bonnets - apart from quarry-stone, these were the principal product of early nineteenth century Swanage [*see entry for Victoria's visit*]. They were made by the women.

Kelly's Directory for 1889 noted the decline of the product:

"There was formerly a trade in straw plait, giving employment to a number of women and children: it was made into baskets, mats and other fancy articles, but the trade has declined considerably of late years."

Swanage: **British Railways locomotive 34105** - in 1973 the Swanage Railway Society's compelling ambition was to acquire the large mainline steam locomotive which used to carry the resort's name on fast passenger runs between Weymouth and Waterloo. *Swanage* had been pulled off Southern Region in the mid-1960s and taken to the scrapyard at Barry Dock, Glamorgan, but along with two hundred other steam engines she was never broken up. She is an unrebuilt Bulleid Pacific class locomotive, British Railways number 34105, with the original streamlined casing covering the boiler. The nameplate was removed before the engine was sent to the breakers and was in the early 1970s moved from a wall at Clapham Transport Museum to a wall at York Transport Museum. The Swanage society was told they could borrow it to cast a copy.

The scrapyard owners, Woodham Bros., offered *Swanage* to the society for £4,000 and value added tax. The society's chairman at that time, Andrew Goltz, was hopeful, and told me:

"The money will be raised by a share issue. The engine looks scrappy now but under the tin box it is in marvellous condition. We have a quote for £25,000 to restore it to mainline use and this would be done by a man who worked for British Rail but is now a freelance based at Didcot."

The locomotive was built in February 1950 and is known to have occasionally operated on the Swanage line as it was photographed there in 1954. In the early 1960s it worked from the Bournemouth sheds and was withdrawn at Eastleigh on 12 October 1964. *Swanage* was hauled from there to Barry in February 1965 by a famous engine of the same class, No 34051 *Winston Churchill*.

Swanage, however, was to be lost to the town. The society placed a deposit on it and struggled to raise another £4,000, against a background of rising scrap values as world metal prices doubled.

The Swanage group failed to meet a deadline and the locomotive was purchased by a consortium representing the Mid-Hants "Watercress Line". This rival project has revived a stretch of the closed track which runs across the Hampshire Downs from Winchester to Alton, and *Swanage* is now based at Alresford station.

Andrew Goltz observed tersely:

"While congratulating the new owners on rescuing 34105 from the scrapheap we regret that our own interest in the locomotive was not respected."

Swanage would return for a special visit to her home town, working in tandem with sister-engine *257 Squadron*, No 34072, an "unrebuilt" Battle of Britain class locomotive, for an "intensive two train service" [20-21 March 1993].

Swanage as a town - though today it appears as a Victorian and Edwardian creation, modern Swanage was only achieved, between 1850 and 1940, by an unco-ordinated but systematic programme of destruction which removed most signs of both senility and charm.

The resort has much older roots and a defence map of the reign of Henry VIII shows Swanage, like Wareham, as a major Dorset coastal town. In the same reign, the historian John Leland wrote:

"From the mouth of Poole Haven, upon the shore by the south-west, is, in a bay about thirteen miles off, a fisher town called Sandwich and there is a pier and a little fresh water."

By the 1600s, a single narrow road, the High Street, wandered away from the shore - above a creek which had silted into a bog and is now completely gone - and for a mile was choked with houses. Here and there an odd building or two lay in the fields beyond. Most disappeared in the conversion to a seaside resort but a good cluster of the old survives around the parish church and mill pond. Yet the pond itself is of more historically recent make, being created around a spring in 1754 and later enlarged.

The first census, taken in 1801, records Swanage, then generally known as Swanwich, as a town of three hundred houses and a population of 1,382. Corfe, on the other hand, was then only half the size with 741 people living in 152 houses. Wareham, like Swanage, managed well over a thousand inhabitants and had 1,627 people in 381 homes. Villages like

Studland, Stoborough and Kimmeridge each had about fifty cottages. The Swanage population had reached 2,100 by the 1871 census and would double in the twentieth century.

The typical Swanage cottage was small and low. Measuring the outside, it had a size of twenty-five feet by eighteen feet with one large room on the ground floor. Rough stone slabs covered the floor - which was often damp. At one side of the room was a pantry, and at the opposite end a large open inglenook fireplace was used for smoking bacon and had a brick oven on the left and a staircase, or sometimes only a ladder, on the right. This led up into the bedroom which was partitioned into two rooms. The ceiling was only six feet high at the level part in the centre and considerably less where it sloped towards the outer walls.

Four such cottages stood at the site of the Town Hall which was built between 1881 and 1883. There the ground fell away to the creek and the only doors to the cottages were at the back. The front bedroom windows were on a level with the High Street and people could look in: the cottages themselves extended three feet into the road. Between two of the cottages was a narrow passage called The Drong, the Dorset dialect word for an alleyway. Facing these were three old cottages on the other side of the road, demolished in 1959.

Swanage Brick Works - pure industrial archaeology survives in daily use at Swanage Brick Works on the edge of the National Trust's Bankes estate at Godlingston (Ordnance Survey map reference SZ 021 803), south of the Purbeck Hills at Ulwell. It is one of the few brickworks still producing hand-made bricks in Britain, with Wealden clays from a hillock a short distance to the north. The works has been in operation more than a hundred years.

The product is superb in texture and colour, with slight irregularities that make for greater character than the standard sameness of the machine-made counterparts. Several distinct shades are produced, using only natural ingredients as the Wealden beds consist of red, purple, brown, blue and green clays, mixed with white, blue, brown and grey sands. These are stacked in heaps in the yard to weather for several months before being mixed for brickmaking.

The technique of hand-moulding bricks is such that the maker leaves his own signature in the form of a pattern of creases in the face of the brick, and at the works they always know who made each one. After drying gently in tunnels for just over a week, during which time each brick loses a pint of water by evaporation, the setters fill their kilns, also by hand. The kilns stack 45,000 bricks and are fired for eighty-five hours, using three thousand gallons of oil, at a temperature approaching 1200 degrees centigrade. It takes ten days for the kilns to cool. The coloration of a brick depends upon its position in the kiln rather than its ingredients. The darkest brick, which the works markets as "Dorset Blue", comes from the hottest part of the kiln. They are extremely hard and dappled blue. The colour is permanent and does not weather out. Light reds predominate towards the bottom of the kiln.

The Swanage Brick and Tile Company Ltd submitted about fifty of their bricks for tests at the Building Research Station. Their conclusions were highly favourable:

"Consideration of the figures for porosity and saturation coefficients [0.49 C/B by twenty-four hours immersion, plus five hours boiling and water cooling] indicates that the bricks submitted should prove resistant to frost even under the severe conditions that obtain in parapets, free standing walls and retaining walls. The soluble salt content of the bricks [0.11 per cent, slight traces only of calcium, sodium, potassium, sulphate] is very low, and their liability to contribute to the formation of efflorescence [leaching of salts] is negligible.

"The bricks submitted were well made and hard burnt. Their compressive strength [4110 lb/square inch mean crushing load] is moderately high for a hand made brick ...

"They are considered to be bricks of good quality."

Swanage Grammar School - in Northbrook Road, with 240 pupils, it was opened on 23 October 1929 by the Earl of Shaftesbury and closed in July 1975. Its Roll of Honour for the Second World War was presented to St Mary's Church. This records the names of Haydn Newman of the Royal Navy; Edward George Brindle of the Royal Marines; John Lewis Henry Mouland of the Fleet Air Arm; Ronald Cecil Parker of the Army; Michael William Cockbaine, Bernard Denness, Stanley James Honour,

Leslie Newman, George Nicol, Arthur Dennis Slade and William Brian Wheelwright of the R.A.F; and civilians Kathleen Winsome Hawkins and Cyril James Smith.

The school dormitories were to the west at Oldfeld House, on the hill at the north end of Walrond Road.

Swanage Pale Ale - made at Gillingham's Malthouse, from the time of the Napoleonic wars. Later known as Panton's Brewery, it was gutted by fire on 8 November 1854.

Owner James Panton rebuilt it, but production ceased after the construction of the railway into the town, and demolition took place in 1893. Swanage Health Centre now stands on the site.

Kelly's Directory of 1889 enthused:

"The properties of the water here are considered as good as those of Burton-on-Trent, as analysed by Doctors Letheby and Graham, and is exclusively used by Messrs. Panton at their brewery, the produce of which has long been characteristically known as 'Swanage Pale Ale'."

Swanage Post Office - moved to its purpose-built premises near the railway station, from the High Street, in 1908. Edwardian Swanage had sixteen postal workers, handling a volume of letters and parcels that was found to be 21,294 items in one sample week.

Late in the eighteenth century, when even Wareham could seem like foreign parts, an old soldier living at Swanage, Jos Rawles, became Purbeck's first postman. His job was to connect Swanage with the main mail network that passed through Wareham. Each Monday, Wednesday and Friday he walked from Swanage to Wareham and called at Kingston and Corfe Castle. On Tuesday, Thursday and Saturday he walked the other way. Mailbags were carried on each journey and letters and papers had to be collected and delivered on the way. The average was twenty-five items of post each day.

Jos Rawles took his job seriously and walked with a pair of loaded pistols slung at his side. Later the horse was an innovation for the postman of 1800 who could then travel to Wareham and back each day. William Masters drove the first mail cart in the 1820s and did extra business by carrying passengers as well. By 1848 the number of items of mail reached a daily average of thirty, but the real stride forward came in 1850, after establishment of the penny post, when a mail coach joined the service. Regular departure and arrival times were maintained - it left Swanage at nine a.m. and was back by three p.m. The next change was the introduction of a coach-and-four, operating from the Red Lion at Wareham, to replace the first mail coach.

Swanage Railway - see entry for **Railway**

Swanage stone port - replaced Ower Quay on the southern shore of Poole Harbour. The reason for this change of location to the other side of Purbeck was that the high-class marble trade had died and in its place a new industry was founded to dig the building stone from the hills between Swanage, Langton Matravers and the cliffs. Marble and its former customers were gone, the workshops that carved effigies lay redundant at Corfe, and the basis of the new business was to export building stone in roughly cut blocks as directly as possible to the world outside.

Swanage Bay lay below the scene of the new operations, and its sheltered shore had encompassed a fishing fleet for centuries - there was no competitor for the port of the revived stone trade. Swanage was the only choice.

Swanage Times - the local newspaper [founded 1821] became a slip-edition of the Dorset County Chronicle [1830-1940]. It then went through several transformations, first with new owner Eric Putnam [1950s] and then merger with the Poole Herald [1960s], though still preserving its identity with its own front and back pages. Times-Herald Newspapers became the Advertiser Series of free newspapers [1980s] and also continued the tradition of a Swanage edition.

Swanage Tramway - the Swanage Pier and Tramway Act, which received royal assent on 8 August 1859, gave Parliamentary consent for a pier at Swanage "and a tramway to connect the stone quarries in the parishes of Langton Matravers and Swanage, with such pier or jetty". The first directors of the pier company were John Mowlem, Edward Castleman,

George Burt, Thomas Randell, George Moore Dixon, Henry Gillingham, Charles Burt, George Evans and William Tomes.

The pier was to be constructed "at or near the north-west corner of a dwelling-house on the shore, commonly called Marine Villa and to terminate in Swanage Bay, nineteen chains, or thereabouts, eastward from the north-west corner of the said dwelling-house".

A ban was imposed on the use of any locomotive, or rope pulleys from a stationary steam engine, on the tramway in the vicinity of the houses at Swanage. Permission was given for Frances Serrell, the widow of Sheffield Serrell, to construct branch tramways through her land. One section of the main tramway, above the town, is described in the act as "the Swanage incline plane".

The rails of the Mowlem and Burt tramway are still embedded in the Swanage seafront pebbles and fork at a set of points to the south of Marine Parade. A length of about two hundred yards of rails survives. A second set of points can be traced to the south of the amusement arcade, by Fortes' and Evans' ice cream stand. This tramway, the Swanage Pier Railway, originally ran along Commercial Road where there is a faded wooden notice, high on a wall, warning: "TO PREVENT ACCIDENTS GOODS MUST NOT BE LEFT ON OR BY THE LINES OF THE TRAMWAY. 1893."

The tramway ran from the 1859-built pier to the bankers of cut stone. Teams of horses pulled carts along the rails to the ships but this pier was in operation for only the closing years of the stone trade in Swanage.

Swanage Water Works - tall and castellated, dated 1886, built as a convincing imitation of a square church tower. The graceful finishing touch is a delightful circular corbelled turret that overhangs from one corner. This is finished off with a ball on top of its miniature spire. The reservoir is now surrounded by a residential area.

Swanwich - the mediaeval name for Swanage, commonly becoming "Sandwich" from the sixteenth century and into smuggling days and causing confusion which I regularly edit out of modern manuscripts, when historians add "Kent" to references that are clearly to somewhere on the Dorset coast.

"Swanawic" is the first recorded Saxon form of the ancient place-name in 877. The origin of the name is probably "herdsmen's dairy farm" but place-name historian A.D. Mills concedes that "swan is equally possible for the first element, in which case the name might mean swannery".

Swanwic House - in Kings Road West, immediately north-east of St Mary's Church, this was the rectory. It is one of the oldest buildings in the town. There is what seems to be mediaeval masonry in the east wall. The north-east side of the old house dates from the seventeenth century and has an inscription to prove it, cut for rector William Rose and probably giving the date of his induction: "1667 W. R. July 10th."

The symmetrical south elevation with its plat-band, architraves and keystone is a Georgian centrepiece of the mid-eighteenth century. Further expansion, adding the west and north-east wings, is of nineteenth century date.

Tatchell - naturalist **Leonard Spencer Tatchell** [1877-1963] of Rockleigh Cottage, Peveril Point (postcode BH19 2AY) is buried in Swanage Cemetery, Washpond Lane, Godlingston. It is a position redolent of lines from his book on *The Heritage of Purbeck* where he wrote that "above, the noble hills into the afterglow of a perfect day illuminating their summits, recall the beautiful words of the 121st Psalm".

Pre-eminently a lepidopterist, Tatchell was an habitual sender and receiver of caterpillars and butterfly eggs. Many packages were none too well packed and any exotic insect found in the postal system at Swanage would be brought to his door.

Ho-You-Fat, an oriental dealer, regularly sent him Morpho butterflies from the Cayenne penal settlement in French Guiana. He then had correspondence with HM Customs in London after their interception of another Chinaman's letter "asking if I was interested in certain drugs".

British experts in butterflies and moths frequently came to his door, and returned to stay for a week most summers, including Richard South, F.W. Frohawk and Edward Step, who produced standard works on their specialities.

"**Tatty greens**" - favourite nineteenth century Swanage expression of insult, for some unknown reason. One of a group of thirty men outside the Ship Hotel [1875], William Saunders, shouted the words at Charles Robinson [born 1853] and kept repeating them. Robinson then hit Saunders with a stick, for which he would be fined £1. The cause of the ill-feeling seems to have been land that the Robinson family had bought, and issued quarriers with a notice to quit.

Another "quarry dispute" took place opposite the Albert the Good Memorial when some men "in fighting mood" kept shouting "Tatty greens" at Mr and Mrs William Trayte of Herston House. That was followed by a fight in the Black Swan and fines of 10 shillings plus 6s 8d costs for each of the two convicted assailants.

"We want to hear no more of the quarry disputes," the magistrate said.

Tilly Whim Caves - south of Swanage, between Durlston Head and Anvil Point (Ordnance Survey map reference SZ 031 770), this is the most easterly survivor of a series of cliff quarries that stretch westwards for five miles. The whole cliff from here to St Alban's Head is sheer, solid stone. At St Alban's, the best seams lie near the top, with secondary reserves found half-way down the cliff face.

The ideal place for a cliff quarry was where the sea had cut across a valley opening. A gallery was then made outwards along the cliff, mid-way down, and inwards along the flank of the hills that held the valley on each side. Winspit and Seacombe are the most extensive examples, but Tilly Whim Caves and Dancing Ledge show the same principle.

Directly below the ceiling of a quarry such as Winspit - where workings spread up the valley on both sides from the sea - was the *underpicking cap*. This was holed by hand or, later, by pneumatic drills, and charges laid. Explosives blasted through two feet of stone and this was cleared. Gunpowder, the black powder of the Middle Ages, was the substance for the charge, and caused much less splintering than modern gelignite. Then work started using wedges, called *gads*, to carefully cut blocks of stone from the bottom of the gash. This stone was removed till the quarry floor was about ten feet below the roof, and the process continued up to about two hundred feet into the hillside with the galleries some twenty-five feet wide.

As the cliff was solid stone, legs of living rock were left to support the hills and these have survived the quarrymen's day. Where the roof was sufficiently strong there are even some great open caverns without any supports.

Usually the legs of untouched stone are square, with sides about three feet wide, and regularly spaced at ten-foot intervals through the galleries. Other supports had to be built up with blocks of stone. The care taken in their size and placing has meant that most of the quarries still stand: but here and there a support has collapsed and the hill fallen to fill the gap. Such rock-falls have closed Tilly Whim caves as a tourist attraction. All the quarries at Winspit and Seacombe are also derelict and deserted, with water constantly dripping from the roof and, now and again, the intrusion of a cow or two lazing in the gloom. Seacombe's quarries have roofs about twelve feet high and are mainly only supported by a few huge pillars.

Blocks of up to fifty tons were taken from the cliffs and cut into manageable sizes. The quantity of the stone was matched by the problem of transport as away from proper roadways and the rail link, the sea was the natural exit from the cliff face. The method used during the peak years of cliff quarrying is shown in a Victorian lithograph of about 1870 depicting Hedbury Quarry, a wide quarry shelf above the sea about halfway between Dancing Ledge and Seacombe. John T. Dean identifies the original painting as an oil by H.G. Wells R.A., whom his grandfather, C.W.T. Dean knew well. This painting was entitled "Purbeck Quarrymen" and included John Dean's maternal great-grandfather, T.C. Lander, with his two sons, Thomas and Albert:

"It is notable in being, I believe, the only truly accurate depicture of cliff quarrying. Wells was an incredible man for detail, and almost dead-centre is a block which is clearly from the *spangles* beds. It also clinches the matter with regard to the use of salvaged timbers from shipwrecks for the making of *whims*. The matter of the delicate sea-going craft is, however, artistic licence. Should the original painting be traced, I would be very much obliged to hear of it."

A *whim* was mounted on the edge of the cliff - this being a normal derrick made of timbers, and similar to those used today for lowering boats into the sea near Portland Bill. Wood for the whim came from the timber of shipwrecks. In the drawing, a ship's wheel was used as the winch and was obviously geared to minute precision for lowering a heavy block of worked stone into a barge waiting on the calm sea below.

The delicacy of this operation, and the fact that the stone barge had then to reach Swanage Bay, shows why the cliff quarries could only function during the summer. The print also shows a stone being worked and the quarry operator, Thomas Chinchen Lander.

Another whim was at Tilly Whim Caves, which was still being worked during the Napoleonic wars. The whim gave the quarry the second part of its unusual name and Tilly was probably the name of the quarry owner. There was also a Tilly Mead in Swanage, between the High Street and what is now Station Road.

Some written record of Tilly Whim has been preserved. The quarry is mentioned in a letter of 13 April 1813:

"There is so much room in this quarry for any assignable number of men to work, and so great a facility, in summer, of shipping the goods, letting them down at once by a crane into the vessel, that men of industry and enterprise ought to command almost the whole market for the species of articles which this quarry produces ... The sort of goods which this quarry yields are of what is called the Portland Purbeck, a sort of freestone; much like the Portland only harder, and much used for buildings in bridges, harbours, fortification walls, troughs, columns, rollers, staddle stones, etc."

Calculations of the output of Tilly Whim have been made from a series of accounts dated between 1805 and 1812. The total production of the quarry for the five-year-period ending on Ladyday in 1810 appears to have been:

37	setts of brigs and caps
14	setts of rick stones
83	pairs of staddle stones
340½	pecks of sinks and troughs
318½	feet of rollers
2305	tons of backing
97	tons of blocks

133   tons of pitchers

The majority of late eighteenth and nineteenth century farm granaries in southern England were built on Dorset staddle or rick- stones. Charles Vancouver reported to the Board of Agriculture from Hampshire in 1813:

"A very excellent practice seems to be fast gaining ground in many parts of the county, of building wheat barns, as well as corn stacks in general, upon stone stands or staddles, the stones, or legs and caps (as they are usually called) are supplied from the quarries of Purbeck and Portland, and cost at the seaports or wharves at the head of the marine navigation, about seven shillings per pair."

Only a small proportion of these granaries survive, but of them some ninety-five per cent have either nine or twelve staddles.

Tilly Whim quotations and the Pentonville pillar - on the sheer cliff above the quarried chambers at Tilly Whim Caves, George Burt had an inscription cut into the stone, in a panel twenty feet above the ground when he opened the caves to the public in 1887:

> THE CLOUD CAP'D TOWERS,
> THE GORGEOUS PALACES,
> THE SOLEMN TEMPLES,
> THE GREAT GLOBE ITSELF.
> YEA, ALL WHICH IT INHABIT
> SHALL DISSOLVE
> AND LIKE THE BASELESS
> FABRIC OF A VISION
> LEAVE NOT A RACK BEHIND
>
> SHAKESPEARE

There had been access difficulties as visitors to Tilly Whim crossed on to a neighbouring estate, but Burt solved the problem in typical fashion:

"Formerly, tourists to the Tilly Whim Caves were obliged to trespass on adjacent lands, but Mr Burt came to the rescue by blasting a subterranean passage deep through the rocks, whose steep descent gives ready access to the rocks and caves. At the entrance to this subterranean passage is a granite column [in three octagonal sections] which now invites to the caves; formerly it 'invited' to the dungeon, for it once stood at the entrance to Pentonville [Prison]! It was erected here in '1887'. Opposite, the wall buttress reads, 'Above sea 102 feet'."

Burt also added an inscription to the wall of the first gallery with its potted history:

"THESE CAVES WERE FORMED CENTURIES AGO BY MEN MAKING SINKS AND RICK-STONES. SMUGGLING WAS ALSO CARRIED OUT HERE, AND BOTH WERE DISCONTINUED ABOUT THE END OF THE FRENCH WARS, 1814."

Rock-falls had closed Burt's dungeon to the public at the time of writing.

Tithe Barn Museum - in the seventeenth century building fifty yards east of St Mary's Church. At the entrance is a London cannon-bollard cast for Christ Church, Middlesex - "CH T. CH MIDDX 1819". Beside the door, a stone records:

"THE TITHE BARN WAS GIVEN TO THE TOWN BY TONY PARSONS TO COMMEMORATE HIS FAMILY, 30 JANUARY 1976."

Its prize exhibit is the **Gibbet Stone**, a heavy, rough-hewn, morticed boulder removed from the top of Court Hill where - at what was the western end of the development line in the High Street until Victorian times - it stood at the entrance to seventeenth century Swanage as a deterrent to rebellion.

The stone is holed in the centre for a wooden shaft, from which an arm would have extended from the top to hold chains and an iron girdle or frame in which a body could be suspended - after being hanged elsewhere on a gallows.

Towards the end of the summer in 1685 the town would have received its gory share of the five victims of Judge Jeffreys' Bloody Assize who were hanged, drawn and quartered at Wareham. This was in the aftermath of the Duke of Monmouth's defeat at the Battle of Sedgemoor and portions of his supporters and their vanquished peasant army were distributed across the western counties to blister and blacken in the sun, as a warning to the populace of the grim price of revolutionary failure.

Toop - the Swanage scandal of 1837, the year of Queen Victoria's accession, was that **John Toop** ran out on his wife Margaret and left her depending on parish funds. The magistrate issued a warrant against him and the town recovered £15 19s 4d.

Tovey - "Sink the *Bismarck*" overlord, **Admiral Sir John Cronyn Tovey** [1885-1971], Commander-in-Chief of the Home Fleet and later Admiral of the Fleet, retired to Swanage after the war. He was created Baron Tovey of Langton Matravers in 1946.

He is buried beneath a large, flat slab in Swanage Cemetery, Washpond Lane, Godlingston:

"JOHN CRONYN/ TOVEY/ ADMIRAL OF/ THE FLEET/ FIRST BARON OF/ LANGTON MATRAVERS/ 12 JANUARY 1971."

Town Hall - built by George Burt on the site of the Drong Cottages in the High Street [1881-83] but with a distinguished frontage that is much older [1670]. Although it has only two storeys, it is still a tall building and the striking feature is the stonework of the frontispiece. This was bought by Burt in London. It had been part of the facade of the old Mercers' Hall, designed by Edward Jerman, though wrongly attributed to Sir Christopher Wren, after the Great Fire of 1666. Building was under the direction of John Oliver. Demolition appears to have taken place in 1860-61.

Among the inscriptions on the walls are "Cheapside 1670" and "Swanage 1882". At the back of the Town Hall is a small rectangular stone building with a stone-slated roof and heavy nail-studded door. The interior is eight feet by ten feet and the single window is small and has an iron grill. This is the Lock-up and a tablet above the doorway reads:

"Erected For the Prevention of Vice & Immorality By the Friends of Religion & good Order A.D. 1803."

This tiny cell, the local prison, was moved from near the parish church. It was erected originally "on the north side of ye Church Tower" but was moved when the church was rebuilt, into the south-west corner of St Mary's churchyard. Boys from the quarries would stand above it, at the top of some steps, and bombard the door with stones when a drunk was locked inside.

Townsend - see entry for **Quarries**

Travers - "building rector" **Rev Duncan Travers** [incumbent 1854-87] masterminded a programme of ecclesiastical and community improvements. Most involved land acquisition and construction works.

First he decided that the extension graveyard across the road from St Mary's was grossly inadequate and set about obtaining the land beside Northbrook Road for the town's main Victorian cemetery [1855].

Then he rebuilt St Mary's Church, leaving only the tower intact, and added a couple of large rooms to Swanwic House which was then the Rectory [1860]. The National School was trebled in size. A coach-house became the parish-room. Herston Schools were extended and the hamlet given its own church of St Mark [1869]. He later installed its "hot water apparatus" [1880] and guided the restoration of the village church at Worth Matravers under the patronage of the Earl of Eldon.

Trocadero - pre-Second World War restaurant, the town's best, at the south end of The Parade (postcode BH19 1DA). This substantial block of three-storey Edwardian shops and flats was erected on the site of the former quarrystone *bankers*.

The fashionable "Troc" specialised in crab and lobster salads and cream teas.

Turks - the epithet of Poole people for Swanage men in the nineteenth century, because of their vulgar roughness and general ignorance of commercial and business conventions.

Those who were Swanage born and lived in Wareham had the nickname *Turkey*. It was originally a stronger insult than it sounds today, the Turks being notorious for cutting off their prisoners' testicles. Some British ex-soldiers travelled the countryside to reveal their mutilation and receive handouts from parish funds.

United Reformed Church - standing on the north side of the High Street, close to its rounded corner with Church Hill. This "Built 1705" and "Rebuilt 1837" frontage is that of the former Congregational Chapel. Its rebuilding was total, by George Gollop of Poole, into the solid, plain upright lines of early Victorian Perpendicular architecture.

The 1837 chapel was later converted to a schoolroom and a new church added on the east side. There is a memorial to its early nineteenth century deacon, Samuel Marsh, who died in 1841.

The foundation stone for the new church "was laid by Stephen Collins, son of the late Mr William Collins, for many years a deacon of this church. August 22nd 1900."

The north wall was blown out, and the organ destroyed, by a wartime German bomb [1943].

Unknown soldiers and sailors - "Known unto God" in Swanage Cemetery, Washpond Lane, Godlingston, are two Merchant Navy men with the same inscription: "A Sailor of the Second World War." Their bodies were recovered on 3 June 1942 and 19 September 1942. A third man, his body washed up on 18 July 1942, has a variation of the inscription on his headstone: "A Sailor of the 1939-45 War."

There is also "A Soldier of the Second World War" with his stone dated 8 July 1944.

Verney Farm - a 150-acre wedge of National Trust land, running alongside the parish's western boundary, with Langton Matravers, south from the Priest's Way (Ordnance Survey map reference SZ 010 782) to the sea. It is mainly coastal limestone downland and is crossed on the seaward slope by Swanage public footpaths number 55 and 26, the latter being the main coast path.

Victoria's visit - young Princess Victoria, four years before she became Queen Victoria [1819-1901, reigned from 1837], came to Swanage on an unexpected royal visit, on 7-8 August 1833. The party stayed at Swanage

Manor, then the Swanage Hotel, and hereafter to be the Royal Victoria Hotel.

Only on the afternoon of 6 August did the town know they were coming, as Rev Thomas Oldfeld Bartlett, the rector, records in his journal for that Tuesday: "News came this afternoon that the Duchess of Kent and her daughter the Princess Victoria would sleep at Swanage Hotel Wednesday night and proceed to Norris Castle, Isle of Wight, in the *Emerald* yacht, towed by one of His Majesty's steamers, the next day."

The yacht, "Dear little *Emerald*," to quote Victoria, was on tow to the Isle of Wight, having snagged a hulk in Plymouth Sound and snapped her mast. This had forced the royal party, who were having a leisurely sailing trip down the South Coast, into an overland retreat by road, leaving Torquay early on the Wednesday and pressing on through Exeter, Honiton, Axminster, Bridport and Dorchester to Wareham, Corfe Castle, Kingston and finally Swanage.

Municipal dignitaries waylaid them with speeches en route. Swanage greeted them with a parade comprising Sunday School children, the town Band, and two Union Clubs of sick-benefit society members, who were hard-drinking quarrymen. They turned out of the White Swan and the Anchor and waited on Court Hill - the entrance to town where the building line of the High Street ended until long into Victoria's reign - for three hours, until the royals arrived at 8.30 in the evening. Dinner was at 9.00.

"We had travelled in all today 105 miles," Victoria wrote in her journal. "I stayed up till near 10. I was soon in bed and asleep. I awoke at 7 and got up at 8. At quarter past nine we breakfasted. At about half-past Mamma received an address from the inhabitants of Swanage. The ladies of Swanage presented me with a straw bonnet, the growth, make and trade of the place."

Then came the inevitable presentations of the good and the great. They were Lady Caroline Marant (sister of Lord Errol); Lady Isabella St John (daughter of the Duke of Grafton); Mrs Dawson Damer (from Came House, Winterborne Came); Lady Caroline Calcraft (wife of John Hales Calcraft MP of Rempstone Hall, between Corfe Castle and Studland).

"At 11," Victoria continues, "we went aboard the *Emerald* to be towed up to Norris."

The Dorset view of the Princess, as seen on an earlier leg of the tour when the party went through Dorchester on their way to stay with the Earl of Ilchester at Melbury House [1 August 1833], was recorded by the Dorset County Chronicle:

"The young Princess, who was the chief object of attraction, stood in the carriage, which was an open travelling barouche, and repeatedly acknowledged in her most engaging manner the attention paid to her. She is a most interesting child, and her countenance denotes the possession of great intellectual powers."

As for the Princess's Swanage bonnet, she was still wearing it on disembarking from the *Emerald* at East Cowes on the Isle of Wight.

Viney - doctor's son **Captain Philip Ernest Viney** [1888-1914] of Cintra, Swanage, and the Leicestershire Regiment "died for England" at Bailleul on 17 December 1914. **Commander Rolf Viney** RNA survived the Great War but died shortly after on 22 April 1922, aged 37. There is also a memorial in St Mary's Church to **J. Ernest Viney** MD, MA who died in 1930, aged 75.

Virginia House - attractive early nineteenth century Purbeck stone town-house, symmetrical with an arched doorway in the middle and smart, tall lines. It stands on the north side of the High Street, on the brow of the hill immediately north-west of the Black Swan.

There is a central datestone halfway up the side of the building, between the two upstairs windows, inscribed "T.C. 1811". The house continues upwards into an exceedingly high attic and a steeply pitched stone slated roof.

Volunteer Camp - in 1868 and 1873, and on into Edwardian times, the full county complement of Dorset Rifle Volunteers held their main annual camp in July beside Swanage Bay at the north end of the town on the eastern fields of Whitecliff Farm. It was a mass of white tents, set out in a dozen rows, with an officers' mess, officers' reading tent, hospital and privates' mess tent, as well as ladies' cloak tent for visitors. The riflemen even brought their own printing press on to the field and produced a camp newspaper, the Swanage Spider. I had heard of its existence and tried for many years to obtain copies, and eventually bought a small batch through the efforts of bookseller Peter Shaw.

This provides some delightful camp gossip as well as the basic background information:

"The field in which the tents are pitched is on a gentle declivity towards the sea, and terminates by a precipitous cliff overlooking the lovely beach. The field, which is about eleven acres in extent, has been kindly lent for the purpose by Mr Isaac White, of White Cliff Flax Mills. Adjoining this is a meadow, also lent by Mr White, in which the sutlers' [camp workers] camp is found; and the drill ground contiguous [immediately to the west] is a large field, seventeen acres in extent, placed at the disposal of the battalion by Mr Samuel Hunt, of Godlingston Farm. The prospect obtained from the camping-ground is magnificent, the cliff which forms a kind of natural gallery around the amphitheatre of the bay, giving a peculiar advantage to the spectator."

The writer notes that the camp field was "an 'alms land' of Ulwell".

On the lighter side, there had been a little difficulty with the Dorset intellect: "Whilst the battalion were drilling yesterday a worthy Sergeant Instructor put the following question to a recruit: What are you, front or rear rank? 'Narne o'nt.' See Johnson's dictionary or somewhere else." Much of its humour cannot outlive the participants. In one of the 1873 issues there is a reference to "the same fat-headed reptile that was prowling about the refreshment tents the first time we camped here, crawled up before the officers and looked smiling upon me, and then he leered at the officers and said: 'This man is not drunk.'" Some knowledge of the politics of the time is a help: "When the Ministers shall have finished their whitebait dinner at Greenwich, and lighted their cigars, what bathing place will the Chancellor of the Exchequer be like." The answer to this - under the heading "Quantum stuff" - is Lowestoft. You need to recall that Robert Lowe was Gladstone's chancellor, and progress to "Lowe stuffed". Much, however, is timeless: "All women ought to be dear to men. Some are - very." Minorities as always were a ready target: "A Black Man Wanted. - If he has a tail he would be preferred. - Apply at Pandemonium, Dorchester line."

Private Charles Powell wrote a song to the tune Auld lang syne, which he entitled The Volunteers are Ready:

> The Volunteers are ready now,
> And wait our country's call
> To boldly go, and beat their foe,
> Or in the struggle fall.
>
> We'll conquer, or we'll die my boys,
> We'll conquer or we'll die;
> Thus freely meet a soldier's death,
> And there in glory die.

It has the famous split infinitive of a century later - the "boldly go" opening television's Star-trek - excused in both cases by euphony. Swanage featured in this fragment from Colour Sergeant E.T. Budden's song to the tune of *Le Petit Tambour*, entitled *The Camp-fire King*:

> Nor would we Swanage Bay forget,
> For boats and bathing rare;
> Nor all the fun of tented life,
> Nor Drew's substantial fare!
>
> Yes, we'll pile up the faggots high,
> And wake the jocund song,
> For the Camp-fire comes but once a year,
> And does not tarry long.

Welles - occasional longevity was also a thing of the past, proved by **Henry Welles** [1516-1607], of Godlingston Manor, whose brass in St Mary's Church, Swanage, records he was "seconde sonne to Thomas Welles of Bradbridge in ye county of South [? being possibly contraction of Southampton] Esqvier who being of the age of 91 departed this life ye 25th of January 1607". The brass is also to "Marie his first wife, sister and heir to John Pole of Godlingstone Esqvier who died in Ano 1560".

Wesley - founder of Methodism **John Wesley** [1703-91] visited Swanage in 1774, 1776 and 1787. The third arrival was enforced.

"We were glad to put into Swanage," he wrote regarding that trip, when a gale forced his ship to take refuge in the bay. It was a sensible precaution but the following day the vessel was nearly lost off Alderney, on the final leg of its risky passage to Guernsey.

The other two visits were by road. The first was in October 1774 at the request of Mary Burt who came in person, having walked the 48 miles to Salisbury to fetch him. She is said to have carried her baby on the walk and to have returned to Swanage in Wesley's chaise. In another version of the tradition she is said to have been accompanied on the walk by two other women, their surnames being Collins and Webber.

Wesley noted after this visit that the Swanage "people in general are plain, artless, good-natured and well-behaved".

The picturesque stone-roofed cottage in the High Street where Wesley stayed was demolished after being damaged by a German bomb. This dropped at 16.30 hours on 14 May 1942 - during the town's 315th alert of the Second World War. A circular commemorative stone inscribed around the edge "JOHN WESLEY'S COTTAGE" and with the date 13 August 1787 at the centre - that of the shelter from the storm but not when he stayed in the cottage - was taken from the debris and put into the garden of Mrs J. Smith at Fontmell Magna, near Shaftesbury.

It was replaced by a stone plaque set into the gatepost of 66 High Street (postcode BH19 2NY) which is believed to be the only surviving trace of the old John Wesley's cottage. This stone was unveiled by Swanage mayor Bryan Hancock [1975] and does, at least, have the correct date: "IN A COTTAGE ON THIS SITE JOHN WESLEY STAYED 12-13 OCTOBER, 1774. THE COTTAGE WAS DESTROYED BY ENEMY ACTION 14 MAY, 1942."

Wesley's second visit was an extension of his trip to Corfe Castle on 5 September 1776. He started there early in the morning, preaching in the open air, and went on at noon "to a large and deeply serious congregation" at Langton Matravers, followed by a "still larger congregation" on a meadow at Swanage in the evening.

The site of Wesley's Cottage was cleared in the late 1980s and the second commemorative stone disappeared in the process. Five stone-built terraced houses were erected [1989]. They are numbers 1 to 5 Wesley Gardens [at 66 High Street].

West End Cottage - see entry for *Thomas Hardy*

The White House - eighteenth and early nineteenth century traditional Swanage stone-built seafront house, run in the first part of the twentieth century by David Hibbs as a guest-house. Later it became tea-rooms, serving during the Second World War as the town's Home Guard headquarters. It is now an information office.

Whitecliff Farm - seventeenth century L-shaped building between the northern suburbs of New Swanage and the slopes of Ballard Down (Ordnance Survey map reference SZ 030 807). Its surrounding land, 222 acres, was bought by the National Trust in 1976, as part of its Enterprise Neptune campaign to save Britain's unspoilt coastline.

It is an ancient settlement site, recorded by the Normans in their Domesday Survey of 1086, and the farm may well have had its main section built in 1683 as a date-stone inscribed with this has been re-set in a barn.

There are also eighteenth century sections of the house and mullioned windows and inglenook fireplaces, some original and others the result of sympathetic reconstruction.

Strip lynchets survive in a poor condition to the north-west (SZ 028 808) in a former open field which used to extend to the foot of Ballard Down. These were mediaeval raised strip fields, worked as cultivation terraces.

The farm occupies the entire north-east corner of the parish and rises to meet even more extensive National Trust lands on Ballard Cliff. [*See also the entries for Ballard Down, Round Barrows and Punfield Cove*]

Wild Wave - an inauspicious name for the Exeter brigantine thrown on to Peveril Point in a gale [23 January 1875]. She balanced on one of the outer ledges, pounded by the ferocious sea that prevented two gigs from attempting a rescue. A rope was fired by rocket from the shore but the stricken vessel then lurched and the line was lost.

Further attempts at saving the crew were prevented by darkness and the conditions but the brigantine was still precariously wedged on the ledge at dawn. Six crewmen were still visible, screaming for help.

This time the gig had more success and came alongside, bouncing up and down with the waves. All were able to jump for safety with only moments to spare. As soon as the rescue was effected the *Wild Wave* slipped for the last time, rolling from the ledge and being claimed by the sea.

The rescue was seen as a miracle and would win the town the allocation of a lifeboat.

Windmill Knap - rising ground at the 200-feet contour just west of Burnham's Lane at Godlingston and above Langton Matravers public footpath number 13 (Ordnance Survey map reference SZ 007 801) has two claims to fame, though there is nothing to be seen on the site today.

The ruins of its tower windmill were visible in Victorian times and reputed to have been built with the stone from a ranger's lodge of the mediaeval Purbeck Forest. Its walls were still standing in 1618 and, as with a similar hunting lodge on Creech Barrow Hill - six miles to the west and which does still have visible foundations - it is said by local legend to have been built by King John.

East of the Knap, the memory of the windmill is also perpetuated by Windmill Barn (SZ 009 800).

Worth Matravers - the mother parish of Swanage, when the latter was a fishing hamlet, in the Middle Ages. Rectors visited their seaside appendage via the Priest's Way, which runs along the stone plateau to the south of Langton Matravers. "The Rectory of Worth with Chapelry of Swanwich [Swanage]" was how it was described.

By 1486, however, Swanage was being listed as the first preference: "The Rectory of Swanwich alias Worth." Then, in 1506, the position was officially reversed to recognise the ascendency of Swanage. It became the mother church, with a rector, and Worth its vicarage, with the clerical appointments there being made by the rector in Swanage.